Philippians and Colossians Quick Study Commentary

Chad Sychtysz

© 2025 Spiritbuilding Publishers.
All rights reserved. No part of this book may be reproduced in any form
without the written permission of the publisher.

Published by
Spiritbuilding Publishers
9700 Ferry Road, Waynesville, Ohio 45068

PHILIPPIANS AND COLOSSIANS
Quick Study Commentary
By Chad Sychtysz

ISBN: 978-1-96480-509-2

Spiritbuilding
PUBLISHERS

spiritbuilding.com

Table of Contents

Quick Study Commentary: Philippians

Introduction to Philippians 1
Section One: Salutation and Opening Comments (1:1–11) 6
Section Two: Expectations of Christian Living (1:12—2:30) 10
    Paul's Proclamation of the Gospel (1:12–20) 10
    Encouragement to Live in a Worthy Manner (1:21—2:4) 14
    The Pre-eminent Example of Christ (2:5–11) 22
    Working Out One's Salvation (2:12–18) 28
    The Coming of Timothy and Epaphroditus (2:19–30) 32
Section Three: The Heavenly Perspective (3:1–21) 35
    Gaining Christ through the Sacrifice of All Things (3:1–11) 35
    Letting Go in Order to Move Forward (3:12–21) 42
Section Four: Reliance upon God (4:1–23) 48
    Dwelling upon Excellence (4:1–9) 48
    The Philippians' Support of Paul (4:10–19) 54
    Final Thoughts and Salutation (4:20–23) 57
Sources Used for Philippians 59

Quick Study Commentary: Colossians

Introduction to Colossians 61
Section One: Salutation and Paul's Praise (1:1–14) 68
    Salutation (1:1–2) 68
    Paul's Prayer on Their Behalf (1:9–14) 71
Section Two: The Divine Nature of Christ (1:15–20) 78
    The Pre-eminence of Christ in the Old Creation (1:15–17) 78
    The New Creation in Christ (1:18–20) 82
Section Three: Standing Firm in Christ (1:21—4:1) 86
    Paul's Ministry to Christ's Gospel (1:21—2:5) 86
    Christ Is the Substance of One's Regeneration (2:6–15) 95

Warnings against Self-imposed Religion (2:16–23) 105
The Transcendent Christian Perspective (3:1–4) 110
The "New Self" (3:5–11) 115
Results of the Transformed Life (3:12–17) 119
Relationships in the Lord (3:18—4:1) 123
Section Four: Final Remarks and Salutations (4:2–18) 128
What Is Expected of Believers (4:2–6) 128
Paul's Personal Circumstances and Salutations (4:7–18) 131
Sources Used for Colossians 135

Scripture taken from the NEW AMERICAN STANDARD BIBLE ®, Copyright © 1960, 1962, 1963, 1968, 1971, 1972, 1973, 1975, 1977, 1995 by The Lockman Foundation. Used by permission.

The author of this workbook can be contacted at chad@booksbychad.com.
Cover design by Larissa Lynch

Introduction to *Philippians*

Philippi was the first Macedonian city into which Paul entered because of what has often called "the Macedonian vision" (Acts 16:11–12). It was built upon the banks of the Gangites River, about ten miles inland from the seaport of Neapolis. Philippi was originally named Crenides in the ancient kingdom of Thrace but was overthrown and re-named by Philip II of Macedon, father of Alexander the Great, in the mid–4th century BC. The city was in an excellent location for a military stronghold, since it guarded the route coming into Macedonia from a sea-based invasion. It was also near gold mines which would eventually provide financial backing for Alexander's march across the world. "Inestimable consequences flowed from this conquest. It has been truly said that if Philip and Alexander had not gone East, Paul and the gospel which he proclaimed could not have come to the West. For, these conquerors brought about the *one* world of Hellenistic speech that made possible the spread of the gospel to many regions."[1]

Historical Background: Philippi became a Roman colony by an edict of Augustus (Octavian) Caesar, in commemoration of his and Antony's victory over Brutus and Cassius (42 BC). "Chief among the assets of Philippi was its status as a Roman colony."[2] A Roman colony was a satellite of Rome itself, and its citizens enjoyed all the rights and privileges as did citizens of Rome. "The colonists [of a Roman city] went out with all the pride of Roman citizens, to represent and reproduce the City [i.e., Rome] in the midst of an alien population."[3] Philippi was free from taxation, had its own city government (rather than being overseen by a provincial ruler), and enjoyed autonomy as long as its own laws did not violate Roman law. It was comprised of three groups: the Roman colonists themselves; the native (Greek) Macedonians; and "a large

---

1 William Hendriksen, *New Testament Commentary: Galatians, Ephesians, etc.* (Grand Rapids: Baker Books, 1995), 5.
2 Pat Edwin Harrell, *The Living Word Commentary: The Letter of Paul to the Philippians* (Austin, TX: R. B. Sweet Co., Inc., 1969), 8.
3 W. J. Conybeare and J. S. Howson, *The Life and Epistles of St. Paul* (Grand Rapids: Eerdmans, 1964), 225; bracketed words are mine.

group of [Eastern] Orientals, including Jews."[4] While its citizens spoke Koine Greek, Latin was Philippi's official language.

On his second missionary journey (ca. AD 52), Paul (and Silas) came to Philippi and sought out a synagogue of Jews, as was his practice in coming to a place that had not yet been evangelized. He found no synagogue, suggesting that there were not enough Jewish men to establish one (which required at least ten heads of households). He did, however, come upon Jewish women who were praying by the river, and to them he preached the gospel of Christ. One woman, Lydia, heard this gospel and obeyed it, and thus became the first known convert to Christianity on the continent of Europe (Acts 16:13–15). After this, however, Paul encountered trouble that is well known to Bible students. A slave-girl who allegedly possessed the ability to divine the future began following Paul and Silas and disclosing their identity as "bond-servants of the Most High God." After "many days" of this, Paul finally had had enough and exorcised from her the demonic spirit that had been the source of this information (Acts 16:16–18). This, of course, ruined the steady income her masters had enjoyed until that moment. They took their anger out on Paul and Silas and dragged them before the city magistrates to face criminal charges. The (implied) charge was that of *religio illicita* ("illegal religion") since it was against Roman law to introduce an entirely new religion to any imperial city or territory. The other charge was that of disrupting the peace of the city. These charges were based upon spite and ignorance, since these men did not know or understand the gospel message that Paul preached. Nonetheless, the city officials had Paul and Silas beaten and imprisoned (Acts 16:19–24). Later, after the city officials found out that these evangelists were Roman citizens, they feared severe repercussions from Rome and begged that Paul and Silas leave them—which they did, but in their own time (Acts 16:35–40).

After this, Paul later visited Philippi again, and enjoyed a very favorable relationship with the church there. These were good people of solid

---

4   H. I. Hester, *The Heart of the New Testament* (Liberty, MO: Quality Press, Inc., 1963), 282; bracketed word is mine.

character. "The men were manly, the women womanly; and like the centurions so often mentioned in the NT, many of them with military background exhibited the stern qualities of rugged dependability, honesty, liberality and faithfulness."[5] The Christians at Philippi were extremely supportive of Paul and were among those who gave even to their own hurt because they first gave themselves to the Lord (see 2 Cor. 8:1–5, Phil. 4:15–16).

Authorship: There is virtually no doubt that Paul wrote *Philippians*.[6] The personality of the author is consistent with everything we know about Paul; furthermore, his name is in the salutation. "This letter is so fresh, distinct, [and] inimitable in every way that forgery is impossible."[7] It is clear from internal evidence that Paul was in Roman prison at the time of writing but expected to be released soon (1:12–14, 2:17–28). There is no good reason to believe that this imprisonment was other than that which Luke mentioned at the end of *Acts*, where Paul spent "two full years" in prison while waiting for his official hearing before Emperor Nero (Acts 28:30–31). Given this premise, the writing is dated ca. AD 62, or about ten years after the founding of the church in Philippi. This letter was carried from Rome to Philippi by Epaphroditus, who had been sick for some time while he was with Paul (2:25–26).[8]

---

5   James B. Coffman, *Commentary on Galatians, Ephesians, Philippians, Colossians* (Austin, TX: Firm Foundation, 1977), 251.

6   "[Modern attempts] have been made to question the Pauline authorship of Philippians on the grounds of discrepancies, but such efforts have been largely unconvincing. The fact remains that there are no compelling reasons, either within or without the epistle, to doubt the Pauline authorship" (Harrell, TLWC, 14; bracketed words are mine).

7   R. C. H. Lenski, *The Interpretation of Paul's Epistles to the Philippians, Colossians, etc.* (Peabody, MA: Hendrickson Publishers, 1998), 698; bracketed word is mine.

8   "It is rather significant that in a number of such instances in the New Testament, the Apostles, who could have miraculously healed, did not do so in such cases, and these instances emphasize that the Divine powers which God had given them to confirm the gospel never were used for personal, private or selfish reasons" (Roy E. Cogdill, *The New Testament: Book by Book* [Marion, IN: Cogdill Foundation, 1975], 80).

Purpose and Theme: The return of Epaphroditus gave Paul an opportunity to bring the Philippians up to date on his own circumstances, since they were concerned for him. This also provided an excellent occasion for Paul to express his deep gratitude for the gift(s) they had sent to him during his imprisonment. "One of the greatest sources of encouragement to Paul in these dark days of imprisonment in Rome was the sympathetic concern of some of his churches for him. The church at Philippi was not only one of the best of these but was composed of Christians who deeply and genuinely loved Paul."[9] Paul also took this opportunity to impart to them whatever counsel, encouragement, and perspective he could provide as an apostle of Jesus Christ. These combined factors resulted in one of the more personal and letter–like writings of the New Testament (NT).

Rejoicing is a major theme of this epistle, and Paul wanted these people to find joy and cause for rejoicing even amid difficult circumstances (just as Paul did himself, even while in prison). "Joy is the music that runs through this epistle, the sunshine that spreads over all of it. The whole epistle radiates joy and happiness."[10] The implication seems to be: if we (Christians) can rejoice during times of difficulty, we will learn to be joyful and content people in any circumstance (4:11–13). Thus, commentators often refer to Paul as the "optimistic prisoner" from this epistle.[11] "It breathes the language of a father, rather than the authority of an apostle; the entreaties of a tender friend, rather than the commands of one in authority. It expresses the affections of a man who felt that he might be near death, and who tenderly loved them; and it will be, to all ages, a model of affectionate counsel and advice."[12]

Philippi served as the retirement settlement for Roman officers and career soldiers. For this reason, and because of its Roman colony status, it was stable, disciplined, and relatively peaceful. Likewise, the internal

---

9   Hester, *The Heart of the New Testament*, 320.
10   Lenski, *Interpretation*, 691.
11   Hendriksen, *NTC*, 38.
12   Albert Barnes, *Barnes' Notes* (Grand Rapids: Baker Book House, no date), "Introduction," cxl.

character of the church itself was virtually trouble-free. This did not mean it did not have external challenges, however, such as those of the "false circumcision" (3:2-3)—i.e., Judaizing teachers—who tried to infiltrate any of the early churches. One scholar believes that Paul and the Philippians both suffered also from Roman pressure or persecution (citing 1:30). This, he argues, explains references to "citizenship" and Paul's use of "Lord" [Greek, *kyrios*] and "Savior" [Greek, *soter*], which were titles also given to Emperor Nero.[13] In a more natural perspective, while the city prided itself on its Roman citizenship, Paul brought the Christians' attention to a far greater citizenship—that of heaven itself (3:20-21). In view of this, a "forgetting what lies behind and reaching forward to what lies ahead" theme (3:13) predominates this epistle.

General Outline of *Philippians*

- **Section One: Salutation and Opening Comments (1:1-11)**
- **Section Two: Expectations of Christian Living (1:12—2:30)**
    - Paul's Proclamation of the Gospel (1:12-20)
    - Encouragement to Live in a Worthy Manner (1:21—2:4)
    - The Pre-eminent Example of Christ (2:5-11)
    - Working Out One's Salvation (2:12-18)
    - The Coming of Timothy and Epaphroditus (2:19-30)
- **Section Three: The Heavenly Perspective (3:1-21)**
    - Gaining Christ through the Sacrifice of All Things (3:1-11)
    - Letting Go in Order to Move Forward (3:12-21)
- **Section Four: Reliance upon God (4:1-23)**
    - Dwelling upon Excellence (4:1-9)
    - The Philippians' Support of Paul (4:10-19)
    - Final Thoughts and Salutation (4:20-23)

---

[13] Paul Barnett, *Jesus & the Rise of Early Christianity* (Downers Grove, IL: InterVarsity Press, 1999), 332-3. William Hendriksen also supports this view to some extent (*NTC*, 8).

SECTION ONE:
SALUTATION AND OPENING COMMENTS
(PHIL. 1:1–11)

Salutation (1:1–2): While the opening salutation is from both Paul and Timothy, Paul is clearly the writer of this epistle and the authority behind its content (1:1). The Philippians are well-acquainted with Timothy since he was with Paul when he founded the church there (Acts 16:1–10). At the time of writing, Timothy is accompanying Paul while he is in prison in Rome awaiting his trial before Emperor Nero. "Bond-servants" [Greek, *doulos*] indicates their humble position relative to Christ's own: He is the head of His church, and they are merely His servants. The exclusion of Paul's usual reference to his apostolic authority indicates that he is not writing to them to address problems, but that this is a more personal letter.[14]

"To all the saints … including the overseers and deacons" is a unique address among the NT epistles. In the earliest days, church leadership came directly from the apostles; as time went on, however, this leadership was turned over to the appointed elders and deacons of each congregation. (Note the plurality of men in both groups.) In *Philippians*, however, Paul speaks to the entire group as one. "Saints" [lit., holy ones] are those who are in Christ. "Overseers" [Greek, *episkopois*] is another word for elders or pastors (shepherds) (1 Tim. 3:1–7). "Deacons" [Greek, *diakonois*] are appointed servants who serve the church that appointed them (1 Tim. 3:8–13). "Grace to you and peace" (1:2) is Paul's standard but sincere opening for many of his epistles. The source of all divine grace and spiritual peace is God the Father and His Son, Jesus Christ.

Praise and Prayers for the Philippians (1:3–11): Paul's daily prayers regularly included his gratitude and appreciate for the church in Philippi,

---

14 In this opening, Paul does not refer to himself as an apostle. Yet, "Paul is not dropping his apostolic authority for the time being, he is now only not making it felt" (Lenski, *Interpretation*, 699).

as well as for other churches (1:3–5; see 1 Cor. 1:4, Eph. 1:15–16, Col. 1:3–4, etc.).[15] Despite his lengthy imprisonment, Paul is particularly joyful and upbeat when speaking of the Philippians, partly out of sheer relief that they are relatively trouble free for the moment. He addresses a group that neither divided nor fractured but is striving for unity (1:4). Also, the Philippians are not merely hearers of the gospel but are doers as well (1:5; see James 1:21–25). They take seriously their responsibility as fellow participants in the work of the kingdom, contributing financially to the needs of the saints abroad, and supporting Paul personally in his ministry to the churches. Thus, they do all things for the sake of the gospel, making them fellow partakers of it (1 Cor. 9:23). Thus, "participation" necessarily implies "fellowship"[16]: a special relationship that God created in His church for the very purpose of disciples of the Master working together for a singular cause.

Paul then expresses his confidence that God is actively at work within the church at Philippi (1:6). "God … is not like men. Men conduct *experiments*, but God carries out a *plan*."[17] God never starts something that He does not intend to finish, yet the completion of this work requires the ongoing faith of those in whom He is working. Thus, Paul implies (as he will say directly later) that the Philippians need to continue in their faith so that God will continue to carry out His will in them. Given this, His divine activity has no limits, and will continue until Christ's literal appearance.[18] Paul feels comfortable speaking so

---

15   "A melody is being composed by the apostle in these first few verses which is not readily apparent in translations. In the second verse he spoke of 'grace' (*charis*), in this [third] verse he speaks of 'thank(s)' (*eucharisto*), and in the next verse he will speak of 'joy' (*charas*). As the melody is developed it is to be a joyous song" (Harrell, *TLWC*, 48).

16   The word "participation" (1:5) is from the Greek *koinonia*, which implies a partnership, fellowship, sharing, and/or contribution (James Strong, *Strong's Talking Greek–Hebrew Dictionary,* electronic edition [database © WORDsearch Corp.], G2842). "It is important to note that however the word is translated the basic meaning is always the 'sharing of something'" (Harrell, *TLWC*, 51).

17   Hendriksen, *NTC*, 55.

18   "The day of Christ Jesus" and "the day of the Lord" in NT epistles consistently refers to the Second Coming; see 1 Thess. 5:2, 2 Thess. 2:1–2, and 2 Peter 3:10, for example.

candidly about the Philippians in this way, since he and they have mutual regard and affection for one another ("I have you in my heart") (1:7). His ministry to them and their support of his own ministry—despite all the trials and difficulties involved in both cases—have created a strong bond between the two. The church in Philippi witnessed Paul and Silas' unjust imprisonment for their sakes (Acts 16:22ff) and is aware of Paul's present imprisonment in Rome for the sake of the gospel. Likewise, his love for them is pure and genuine—so much so, that he calls upon God to be a witness of it (1:8).[19]

Paul's prayers for the Philippians include an appeal on their behalf for increasing love and wisdom (1:9).[20] "Real knowledge" implies an increasingly *improved* knowledge—learning that is continuously refined and made more accurate through prayer and study. "All discernment" involves wisdom in dealing with spiritual matters, which includes the ability to judge between right and wrong (Heb. 5:14). The purpose for this knowledge and discernment is then stated (in 1:10–11).

- ❏ **"to approve of the things that are excellent"**: Excellent things must be properly appraised; the natural man of the world does not value them in the way that a spiritual child of God does (1 Cor. 2:11–14). Christians are to "proclaim the excellencies of Him who called [us] out of darkness into His marvelous light" (1 Peter 2:9), but we must first know what these excellencies are to proclaim them. The standard for this approval is the word of God; the application of this approval is in the Christ-like way we live.
- ❏ **"sincere and blameless"**: The Greek word for "sincere" literally means "(to be) judged by sunlight," that is, to be held up to the sun's rays and scrutinized for purity.[21] In the case of believers, we are held up to God's word and exposed by the Light for what (and

---

19 "Affection" (1:8) "literally means 'viscera,' which is a collective term for the internal organs, such as the heart, liver, and lungs, as contrasted with the intestines. The Greeks viewed these organs as the seat of the emotions" (Harrell, *TLWC*, 55).

20 For further exposition on this point, see comments in this workbook on Col. 1:9–10.

21 *Thayer's Greek-English Lexicon*, electronic edition (database © 2014 by WORDsearch Corp.), G1506.

who) we really are (Eph. 5:7–13). If our character is consistent with God's expectations, we are sincere; if not, then we fail the test (2 Cor. 13:5). "Blameless" means "unoffensive," as in not bringing offense against God with our actions, and thus not incurring guilt and His condemnation. This does not mean that we are unable to sin, but that *when* we sin, we take the proper recourse and seek God's forgiveness (Col. 1:22, 1 John 2:1–2). "[U]ntil the day of Christ" indicates the duration of our seeking to be sincere and blameless: until death or the Second Coming, whichever comes first. (This phrase, "until the day of Christ," can also mean "with a view toward the day of Christ." Regardless, the objective and process remain the same.)

- **"having been filled with the fruit of righteousness"**: The power (or producing energy) of this fruit is the Holy Spirit; the believer's connection to this power is his fellowship with Christ. "Paul wants all the Philippians to appear then as being filled with nothing but fruit of a righteous quality."[22] We are made to think of the vine-branch analogy in John 15:1–9: because of our branch-like connection to the Vine (Christ), we can bear fruit (by the Holy Spirit; see Gal. 5:22–23). Thus, the effect of fruit-bearing comes "through Jesus Christ," and is impossible apart from Him (John 15:5).

"[T]o the glory and praise of God" describes the ultimate benefit of this fruit-bearing process: not only do we receive salvation, but God is honored by our decision to serve Him.

Passages such as this (1:10–11) illustrate the full purpose of what Christians do and why we do it. While the world stumbles into the future without purpose, objective, or an accurate understanding of what is to come, the Christian is to be informed, prepared, and looking forward to the full revelation of God's plan in the hereafter. It takes strong conviction to believe in things we have never seen, which is why "we walk by faith and not by sight" (2 Cor. 5:7).

---

22 Lenski, *Interpretation*, 720.

Section Two:
Expectations of Christian Living
(1:12—2:30)

Paul's Proclamation of the Gospel
(Phil. 1:12–20)

It might appear to the Philippians (and anyone else) that Paul's lengthy imprisonment has severely curtailed his efforts to teach and spread the gospel. Yet, Paul holds a different perspective, in part from his own evangelistic experiences. Instead of being a closed door, his imprisonment has opened the door to those who might have never heard the gospel otherwise (1:12). The "greater progress [or furtherance]" of the gospel indicates a pioneering direction that had not yet been taken. Thus, his circumstances have proven to be profitable for the cause of Christ (1:13). The "praetorian guard" (of the governor's palace) refers to the elite Roman guard that directly serves the emperor and provides for his personal safety.[23] ("Praetor" is Latin for "commander-in-chief.") These men are stationed in a special barracks in the actual palace of the emperor, whereas the rest of the soldiers are stationed outside the city.[24] This means that Paul is in a far more comfortable environment than before and has better proximity to Roman officials than he has ever had. "[A]nd to everyone else" indicates a wide array of access and opportunity to share the gospel. Furthermore, because of Paul's presence in the praetorian guard, "most of the brethren" in Rome are emboldened to speak of the gospel more than they might have done otherwise

---

23 "There were originally ten thousand of these picked soldiers, concentrated in Rome by [Emperor] Tiberius. They had double pay and special privileges and became so powerful that emperors had to court their favour. Paul had contact with one after another of these soldiers" (A. T. Robertson, *Word Pictures in the New Testament*, vol. 4 [Grand Rapids: Baker Book House, no date; orig. published 1931], 438; bracketed word is mine).

24 Robert Jamieson, Andrew Fausset, and David Brown, *Jamieson, Fausset, and Brown Commentary: Commentary Critical and Explanatory on the Whole Bible* (1871) (database © 2012 by WORDsearch Corp.), on 1:13.

(1:14). They had someone on the inside, so to speak, opening doors and providing influence for them. As Lipscomb observes, "Courage as well as fear is contagious."[25]

Some Christians, however, "are preaching Christ even from envy and strife" (1:15). Likely, this refers to those Jewish Christians seeking to draw attention to themselves rather than allowing believers to sympathize with Paul and his circumstances. These men may have disparaged Paul's character ("If he were completely genuine, then why has he been sitting in prison for so long?") to magnify their own ("Since I am not being imprisoned, God looks more favorably upon me"). Thus, they envy Paul and strive against him rather than cooperate with him in their ministries.[26] Thankfully, not all believers have responded this way: "some [are preaching] from good will." These brethren act out of brotherly love for Paul, as well as a godly love for reaching the lost (1:16). They understand and respect Paul's apostolic appointment to defend the gospel (Acts 9:15–16, Rom. 1:1–6). The others, however, seek to take advantage of his humiliating circumstances for their self-promotion. They preach the gospel of Christ—at least its *design*, but not its *love*—but they do so for the wrong reason and with impure motives, hoping to further diminish Paul's apostolic influence in the churches (1:17).

"What then?" (1:18)—or "How should I to respond to this?" In Paul's humble view, the preaching of the message of Christ is more important than having his character vindicated by other men. God Himself appointed Paul to be a steward of the gospel, and he answered to Him directly (1 Cor. 4:1–4). In the end, God will vindicate him; under

---

[25] David Lipscomb, *A Commentary on the New Testament Epistles, volume IV: Ephesians, Philippians and Colossians*, J. W. Shepherd, ed. (Nashville: Gospel Advocate Co., 1976), 162.

[26] J. W. Shepherd (in Lipscomb's commentary) offers another view: "It is very likely … that the Christians at Rome were without a strong leadership before Paul's coming, and that some of their leaders, jealous of his influence, became personal enemies" (*Commentary*, 163). While this seems plausible enough, it is also without substantiation. Given Paul's repeated tangles with Christian Jews (Judaizers) in other places of the NT, the first scenario seems more natural. Nonetheless, each Bible student is allowed his own opinion here.

the present circumstances, this is unnecessary.[27] Thus, regardless of the motives of those who preach, at least the gospel is *being* preached. This indicates that the transmission of information itself is accurate, even among those who preach it out of selfish ambition.[28] "Christ is proclaimed" is the real objective, and this is reason for rejoicing. On this, Barnes writes: "It would be better to have preachers that were better instructed, or that were more prudent, or that had purer motives, or that held a more perfect system, yet it is much in our world *to have the name of the Redeemer announced in any* way, and even to be told, in the most stammering manner, and from whatever motives, that *man has a Saviour* [sic]. The announcement of that fact in any way may save a soul; but ignorance of it could save none."[29] Paul's cheerful attitude, despite the ugly way he has been treated by his own brethren, is remarkable and inspiring.

At the time of writing, Paul had been in Roman custody for about two years. This long, grueling ordeal is near its end, however, and no doubt this fact contributes to his positive outlook on his ministry. His comments indicate confidence that he will soon be released, and he credits this prospect not only to God's providence but also the many prayers offered by the Philippian Christians on his behalf (1:19). On the other hand, "deliverance" carries another sense: God may deliver Paul from prison to continue his apostolic ministry, or He may deliver him from this life altogether—i.e., face execution by decree of Emperor Nero—to be with Christ. On "provision [or, supply]," JFB Commentary says:

---

[27] Paul did vindicate himself, to the extent that was necessary, in the Second Epistle to the Corinthians. For a full discussion on his defense, and why he chose to engage in it, see *2 Corinthians Commentary* (Spiritbuilding Publishers); go to www.spiritbuilding.com/chad.

[28] "Apparently the content of these sermons was similar to Paul's preaching and did not contain such false teaching as Judaizers were bringing to Galatia (Gal. 1:6–8). Their basic error was in motive and not in doctrine" (JFB, *Commentary* [electronic], on 1:18).

[29] Barnes, *Barnes' Notes*, 153; emphases are his.

The Greek word for "supply" (*epichorēgia*) was used to describe the supply a choir manager would provide all the members of a Greek choir (who performed in the Greek plays). In short, he took care of all their living expenses. The word then came to mean a full supply of any kind. Paul was looking forward to getting a full supply of Jesus Christ's Spirit as a result of the Philippians' prayer.[30]

The phrase "Spirit of Jesus Christ" is unique in the NT. This is not a different "Spirit" than the Holy Spirit of God but is the same (Rom. 8:9). The Holy Spirit, then, is "of God" as He is "of Jesus Christ," yet He remains one Spirit and an individual personality of the Godhead (Eph. 4:4).[31] "[A]ccording to my earnest expectation … " (1:20)—the Greek word here indicates someone turning his head to see something important.[32] Paul eagerly anticipates that Christ will not allow him to be "put to shame" (or, have any cause for regret) for what he has suffered in His name (2 Tim. 1:12). Instead, he rightly believes that Christ will glorify His name through himself (see John 12:28 and 2 Cor. 4:10). "[W]hether by life or by death" does not mean he has no knowledge of the outcome of his imprisonment (see 1:24–25), but that Christ will be honored through him regardless of that outcome.

---

30 JFB, *Commentary* (electronic), on 1:19. The same Greek word is used in 2 Peter 1:5–7 regarding the "supplying" of one's faith with the different virtues Peter mentions.

31 For an in-depth study of the Holy Spirit, I recommend my book, *The Holy Spirit of God: A Biblical Perspective* (Spiritbuilding Publishers, 2010); go to www.spiritbuilding.com/chad.

32 Thayer, *Lexicon* (electronic), G603.

Encouragement to Live in a Worthy Manner (Phil. 1:21—2:4)

Having described his circumstances, Paul now uses these to draw practical lessons for the Philippian Christians. "For to me, to live is Christ and to die is gain" (1:21)—this is perhaps one of the most well-known verses in this epistle, serving also as an excellent summary of the Christian's perspective.[33] Regardless of whether Paul lives or dies, Christ is the object of his adoration; whatever the outcome, faith in Him works to a beneficial end. To "die" in the Greek (here) indicates an accomplished action; thus, it does not refer to the dying process, but what happens after death. If Paul remains upon this earth, he will continue to serve Christ and fulfill his ministry to Him; if he leaves this earth, he will forever be with the One whom he has loved for so long (1:22).

A Difficult Dilemma (1:23–26): But Paul admits he does "not know which to choose"—this does not mean that he has the luxury *of* choosing, but that he does not know which outcome will be in the best interest of all parties involved. We see him weighing out both sides in his mind (1:23). Certainly, to be with Christ would be "very much better" than to remain here on this earth, but Paul's heart is also with the Philippians and many others who would spiritually profit from the continuation of his ministry.[34] Having considered both prospects,

---

33 "In Shakespeare's *Hamlet*, the Prince of Denmark delivered a soliloquy in which he viewed both the present life and the after-death state as equally undesirable and terrifying. When considering the evils of life, he could incline toward death, except for the soul-shattering thought that evil dreams would torture him. Thus Hamlet stands as the typical unregenerated man, oppressed by life, but afraid to die. Here, the matchless Paul rises above such a dilemma, viewing both life and death as the means of magnifying the Lord Jesus" (Coffman, *Commentary*, 270).

34 It is interesting to note how Paul views life after death. While he does not describe the scene or circumstances of heaven itself, he consistently talks about being "with the Lord" immediately after death (see 2 Cor. 5:6–8). This view does not conflict with our biblical understanding of the resurrection (1 Thess. 4:13–17) but indicates there are details about the believer's life after death we simply cannot know because God has not revealed them. One thing is certain: we cannot impose earthly time, conditions, or limitations upon the heavenly world in which God lives and to which the souls of believers

Paul selflessly accepts what he knows to be the case: he will "remain on in the flesh" for the benefit of the church and the spread of the gospel (1:24).[35] "Convinced" of this fact, Paul looks forward to contributing to the Philippians' progress and their collective "joy in the faith" (1:25). This serves as a positive answer to their prayers and is the basis for their "proud confidence" that they have in him (1:26). It is Paul's full intention to come to Philippi sometime soon after his release from Roman imprisonment. Thus, both Paul and the Philippians will be filled with joy upon seeing the will of Christ being carried out to their own benefit.

The Philippians' Expected Conduct (1:27–30): Regardless of whether he does come to them, Paul admonishes the Philippians to live as godly people. "Only conduct yourselves in a worthy manner of the gospel of Christ" (1:27) follows a familiar theme throughout Paul's epistles: one's association with Christ demands personal responsibility and spiritual integrity (Eph. 4:1, Col. 1:10, 1 Thess. 2:12, etc.). "The conduct of this united band of believers in the gospel is to match the blessed saving gifts they have received."[36] Furthermore, Paul wants to hear that they are "standing firm" and "striving together" for the faith. "Standing" refers to a grounded, stabilized position (see Col. 2:6–7), as opposed to slipping, backsliding, or falling. To "strive together" indicates a cooperative effort toward a singular objective, rather than striving *against* one another (as in 1 Cor. 3:3). Christians cannot reach these positive objectives unless they are:

---

are taken. "This possibility of being with Christ must have been open to an immediate fulfillment or else it would present no real option. There is no room for any concept of 'soul sleeping,' the view that man exists without consciousness until the resurrection, in this passage for the simple reason that the alternatives of being active with the Philippians and unconsciously inactive hardly presents a choice. The prospect of being with Christ, however, is exciting" (Harrell, *TLWC*, 73–4).

35 "Paul is not flattering himself as though his readers still need him. He says only that he is confident they do, and he describes in what respect he thinks they do. He was in a correct position to know, and we know that he judged correctly, that the Lord did let him remain on for a few years. Then came his second and fatal imprisonment, during which he wrote in an entirely different way (II Tim. 4:6–8)" (Lenski, *Interpretation*, 749).

36 Ibid., 752.

- ❏ **conducting themselves in a worthy manner.** The believer's lifestyle must be consistent with the expected behavior of a disciple of the Master. One who claims to "know God" must also be obedient to His commandments (1 John 2:4–6). This also implies that if there is a "worthy" manner, then all "manners" that digress from or contradict *this* one are unworthy and inappropriate.
- ❏ **in one spirit.** This means, united by God's Spirit, even though the word "spirit" here does not specifically refer to Him. People can be united in one *human* spirit to do very bad things (e.g., when the Jews were of one "impulse" to kill Stephen—Acts 7:57), but people who are united with God's Spirit will glorify God and live as His people (1 Cor. 12:3, Eph. 4:3).
- ❏ **with one mind.** While "in one spirit" implies a *spiritual* attitude conditioned by God's own Holy Spirit, "with one mind" indicates people working together for a common goal, as one sports team works together to defeat an opposing team. The "faith of the gospel" is the belief system based upon God's revealed word.

By working together in unity with God's Spirit, the Philippians will have no reason to fear the adversaries of the gospel (1:28).[37] This does not mean that these opponents will not bother them, or that they will not enjoy a measure of apparent success. What it does mean is that believers should not shrink back from walking worthily, standing firm, and striving together because of their fear of these opponents (see Heb. 10:36–39). Paul does not identify the "opponents" here, but later he does warn the church of those of the "false circumcision" (see comments on 3:2–3). "[W]hich is a sign of destruction for them"—i.e., the faith of the gospel will reveal their opponents for what they are—enemies of God—and will speak to their ruin. The "sign [or, evidence]" here may refer to the historical example of all those who persecuted God's people in the past (i.e., in the Old Testament record). None of those antagonists ever escaped divine judgment; they were all destroyed (cf. Deut. 32:35 and 2 Peter 2:3b). Thus, the same gospel serves to vindicate those who

---

37 Who these opponents are, Paul does not say. Lenski (*Interpretation*, 755) believes that Paul refers to the city authorities—the same ones that gave him so much trouble (in Acts 16:19–24). Yet, perhaps a much more general sense is meant, in which "opponents" are all who oppose the doctrine of Christ.

believe in it also condemns those who resist it (2 Cor. 2:14–16, 2 Thess. 1:6–10).

"For to you it has been granted … " (1:29–30)—on the surface, this seems to support the man-made Doctrine of Predestination (a.k.a. Calvinism), in which God allegedly foreordains the spiritual future of every person. Yet, as in every other case where he puts forward the concept of predestination, Paul speaks of the collective of believers (i.e., the church) rather than individual Christians (Rom. 8:29–30, Eph. 1:4–5, 11, etc.). In other words, *the spiritual body of Christ* is predestined (or, "granted" by God) to believe in Him *and* suffer for His name's sake (Rom. 8:16–17). A simple analogy will explain this: suppose you wish to go to Seattle by way of a bus, and so you talk to a certain bus driver. He says, "*This* bus"—referring to the one he operates—"is predestined to go to Seattle." This statement does not refer to what (or how many) people will be on the bus when it leaves, only that the bus is scheduled to go to Seattle. Whether *you* get on his bus does not change this fact. However, once you *are* on his bus, then you too—because of the vehicle you chose, not because you had no decision otherwise—will be going to Seattle. And, if the bus driver were to speak to those who are on the bus as it is *heading* to Seattle, then he could say, "You are all predestined to go to Seattle." This is true because of their present state of *being* rather than something *forced* upon them.

So it is with the church: God has foreordained that His church is headed for glory, regardless of which or how many human souls comprise this church. Whoever is in this church (and remains faithful to its head) will likewise be predestined for glory—not because he had no free will in the matter, but because he is on the only "vehicle" that God will save.

To "believe" in Christ is what Christians do, and to "suffer" for the sake of Christ is what Christians must endure (Mat. 5:10–12, 2 Tim. 1:12). Thus, Paul is saying, in essence, "Remain faithful to the gospel in which you first believed and be willing to suffer for it, yet do not think that your suffering is something unusual or that it destroys the credibility of that gospel" (see 2 Tim. 2:9–10 and 1 Peter 4:12–16 for similar thoughts).

The Mindset of the Believer (2:1–4): "Therefore ... " (2:1) indicates practical conclusions based upon what Paul has already said. If the Philippians are walking rightly, working in unity with God's Spirit, striving together for the gospel, and even suffering for the sake of Christ, then Paul should expect them to be of a certain "mind" or attitude. What follows (2:1–4) does not suggest that the Philippians are thinking otherwise, but Paul's admonition is to *keep on* pursuing a Christ-centered attitude, regardless of their circumstances or the opponents they face.[38] "[I]f there is any encouragement, etc."—more accurately, *since* there are these things, a certain response is expected. The four clauses in this verse (2:1) are conditioned upon actions in the next verse being met (2:2):

- ❏ "encouragement in Christ" indicates any spiritual praise or reinforcement that Christians provide for one another that imitates that which they receive from the Lord.
- ❏ "consolation of love" refers to the comfort or support that Christian love offers when fellow believers act in the best interest of each other (cf. 2 Cor. 1:3–5).
- ❏ "fellowship of the Spirit" means that believers who have communion with Christ also have communion with God's Spirit (2 Cor. 13:14), and that neither of these situations can exist without the other. This phrase can be taken two ways—fellowship *with* the Spirit and fellowship that is learned *from* the Spirit—and either way is fitting.
- ❏ "any affection and compassion" refers to any of the inward feelings that result from a common union with the Lord. "Compassion" can also be (and often is) translated as "mercy" in the NT and refers to the withholding of what one deserves (such as punishment) in anticipation of one's reform. Mercy is virtually always associated with patience, longsuffering, toleration, and forbearance (see Col. 3:12–15).

---

38 This passage (2:1–5) is perhaps one of the most succinct descriptions of the attitude that all Christians ought to demonstrate toward one another. This is an excellent passage to be read before any congregational meeting, business meeting, or any difficult confrontation that Christians must face in dealing with problems in the brotherhood. If every Christian adopts this mindset, then whatever difficulties will arise among brethren will be dealt with quickly, properly, and lovingly.

"[M]ake my joy complete" (2:2) does not mean the Philippians have not yet brought Paul any joy—quite the contrary, he speaks very highly of them (recall 1:3–8). Yet, he wants this joy to reach its fullest extent (1 John 1:4). Thus, while the Philippians have done well so far, he wants them to *continue* doing well (cf. 1 Thess. 4:1). This requires the meeting of conditions that in this passage:

- "same mind"—see comments above on 1:27. This does not mean "same opinions," because fellowship in Christ is not based on human opinions. It does not mean "same conclusions," because an entire group of people can be united in a conclusion that is entirely wrong. Thus, "same mind" requires that that "mind" be set on Christ, and if everyone involved *has* that mind then they will enjoy the fellowship that it produces.
- "same love"—not a selfish or selective love, but one based upon Christ's love for us (John 13:34–35, "as I have loved you"). It is popular for people to define "love" on their own terms and then use *those* terms in their religion. The "same love" to which Paul refers is defined by Christ, not any individual believer, church leadership, or congregation.
- "united in spirit" means what it says: united upon a common element—in this case, God's Holy Spirit—in order to reach a common goal.[39] Thus, Christians' unity is spiritual, not necessarily physical: a congregation—or the entire brotherhood of Christ—does not have to be literally assembled together to be "united," but *does* need to "be diligent to preserve the unity of the Spirit in the bond of peace" (Eph. 4:3).
- "intent on one purpose" indicates that Christians are to focus on something outside of (and bigger than) themselves—a transcendent, heavenly objective rather than a transient or personal one. The unity of inward or spiritual beliefs will be revealed through outward cooperation with those of like beliefs. Those who claim to love Christ, for example, cannot simultaneously withhold love from

---

39 My words are not meant to imply that "one spirit" in this passage literally refers to the Holy Spirit, but that the context of brotherly unity is spiritual in nature, and that this unity can only be accomplished by abiding in God through the written revelation and guidance of His Spirit (John 4:24).

those who belong to Him (1 John 4:20–21). Such inconsistency belies any claims of piety or fellowship with God. On the other hand, when believers focus on Christ, they learn to work together for His sake and will overcome any difficulties they face along the way.

"Selfishness [or, rivalry]" and "empty conceit" have no place in the brotherhood (2:3–4).[40] Such things are the seeds of division, not unity (1 Cor. 1:10). Thus, we are to consider one another with humility (or, lowliness of mind) rather than seeking to please ourselves (Rom. 15:2). Humility—the voluntary *lowering* of oneself while choosing to *raise up* (or defer to) another—is the opposite of pride. Human pride always seeks to exalt itself over another, exert itself against another, or extol itself in the presence of another. Pride always seeks self-gratification at the expense of someone else. Humility, on the other hand, regards others as more important than oneself.[41] (This does not mean that every person *is* more important in every respect, but that this is how the humble person chooses to *treat* him.[42]) If Christ, being the Son of God, can regard us with such dignity and respect, then certainly we who are equals in His sight ought to treat one another with such humility (Rom.

---

40   KJV uses the terms "factions and vainglory." "These twin vices have been spoilers of the church of God in all ages. Petty strivings for place or preferment, jockeyings for advantage, pushing and shoving for prestige or attention—how many congregations of believers in Christ have been blighted or destroyed by the sins Paul mentioned here?" (Coffman, *Commentary*, 276).

41   "Humility … describes the spirit of one who has come to the knowledge of himself in relation to God, and it is, therefore, primarily a Christian grace and not a social virtue. There is no trace in it of the weakness associated with the term in pagan literature. On the contrary, it is the badge of the strong, the first test of a truly great man" (Lipscomb, *Commentary*, 179–180).

42   This addresses the facetious scenario posed by Hendriksen, "How can a man who knows that he is industrious regard the rather lazy fellow-member as being better than himself?" (*NTC*, 100). Lenski responds: "Paul is not asking the impossible or the untrue, namely that I am to think that every other Christian, just because he is a Christian, has more brains, more ability, more everything than I have. Nor does Paul ask that we merely 'consider' one another [as being] above [us] although we know that the facts are quite to the contrary, that a large number are far beneath us" (*Interpretation*, 767; bracketed words are mine). Paul speaks of the order of the giving of attention—"This other person first, and then myself"—not the comparative value or worth of the one to whom the attention is given.

12:10). Instead of seeking to promote our own views, our own agendas, or our own good points, we are to consider the interests of others first.

The Pre-eminent Example of Christ (Phil. 2:5–11)

Whatever disposition Paul requires of the Philippians is drawn from the pre–eminent example of the Master (Christ)—thus, "Have [His] attitude in yourselves [or, Let {His} mind be within you]" (2:5). The believer is not only to take on Christ's name, but also (to the best of his ability) His *heart*. This necessarily demands a proper attitude toward those who also belong to Him. Christ voluntarily chose to humble Himself for the sake of others on a level that exceeds human comprehension, since He (a divine Being) lowered Himself to human life (2:6ff). If the Lord can do this for us who are so undeserving, then *how much more* should Christians do this for each other, especially when we are all equals (both as humans and brethren)?[43]

Christ "Emptied" Himself (2:6–8): In His pre–incarnate life, Jesus existed as a divine Personage of the Godhead (2:6; see John 1:1–3). While it is incorrect to identify Jesus as "the Father," it is entirely accurate to say that Jesus was (is) "God." This means both He and the Father share the same divine nature; they are both uncreated, eternal, and sovereign beings that are above the Creation in every respect. Equality (or unity) *with* the Father is not to be confused with having the exact same identity *as* the Father (John 10:30). God the Father has His identity; God the Son has His own separate identity; yet both are divine Personages of the triune "God" (or Godhead). If you struggle to wrap your head around all of this, you are not alone. We are not meant to fully comprehend all this; we are only to believe that it is *real* and *true*.

Before Jesus stepped into the physical Creation, He embodied (in His pre–incarnate existence) the essential nature and character of God. ("Incarnate" means "in the flesh"—see John 1:14.) He "did not regard

---

43   This section (2:6–11) is referred to by some scholars as "the Christological hymn" (Harrell, *TLWC*, 87–89), which recounts in brief but potent language Christ's mission from His pre-existence with the Father to His triumphant return to the Father, His having completed all the work which the Father gave Him to do (John 17:4–5).

equality with God a thing to be grasped"—i.e., it was not wrong for Christ to regard Himself as equal to God (see John 5:18–24); it was also not wrong for Him to divest Himself of His heavenly glory in order to serve as our Redeemer.[44] It was necessary that Jesus be identified literally with those whom He came to save, as the following passages indicate:

- "And the Word became flesh, and dwelt among us, and we saw His glory, glory as of the only begotten from the Father, full of grace and truth" (John 1:14).
- "For what the Law could not do, weak as it was through the flesh, God did: sending His own Son in the likeness of sinful flesh and as an offering for sin, He condemned sin in the flesh … " (Rom. 8:3).
- "He [God] made Him [Jesus] who knew no sin to be sin on our behalf, so that we might become the righteousness of God in Him" (2 Cor. 5:21, bracketed words added).
- "But we do see Him who was made for a little while lower than the angels, namely, Jesus, because of the suffering of death crowned with glory and honor, so that by the grace of God He might taste death for everyone. For it was fitting for Him, for whom are all things, and through whom are all things, in bringing many sons to glory, to perfect the author of their salvation through sufferings" (Heb. 2:9–10).
- "For we do not have a high priest who cannot sympathize with our weaknesses, but One who has been tempted in all things as we are, yet without sin" (Heb. 4:15).

Christ did not need to continue to "grasp" onto (or, continue to cling to or maintain) His divine glory. At the same time, we could not have grasped His glory—or His role as our sacrificial Lamb—if He had come to us in His heavenly state of being. It is wrong to claim that Jesus gave

---

44 The word "grasped" can be translated "robbery," leading to the awkward KJV translation: " … thought it not robbery to be equal with God." What this passage does mean is "that Jesus did not need to snatch at equality with God, because he had it as a right" (William Barclay, quoted in Coffman, *Commentary*, 281). Another phrasing: "The meaning of the statement is that Christ turned his back on the 'rank' of equality with God, refusing to exert himself for what was his by right, choosing rather the way of obedience" (Harrell, *TLWC*, 90).

up being God to become human, since this was not necessary and did not happen. It is accurate to say that when Jesus became a Man, He did not cease to be God. This is impossible for us to understand; it is like saying, "The apple became an orange without ceasing to be an apple."[45] Yet, it was necessary that God (in the Person of Christ) die for His Creation, since no one else could provide the atonement necessary for human sin. Thus, "He emptied Himself" (2:7)—i.e., Christ divested Himself of His heavenly privileges, but not His essential nature.[46] He voluntarily relinquished—for the purpose that His coming to us "in the flesh" required—the rights and honor He deserved as the Creator (John 17:4, Col. 1:15–17) to save His Creation. He took on the form of an earthly "bond–servant" rather than retain His heavenly "form of God," the One worthy of being served.[47] Not only this, but He took upon Himself "the likeness of men," which was an unfathomable step downward from His equality with God.

---

45 "Paul simply states the fact; he does not philosophize about its possibility. Facts are facts whether Paul or we are able to understand their possibility or not" (Lenski, *Interpretation*, 780).

46 "Emptied Himself" cannot mean "He ceased to be God," whether partially or fully. "Of what did Christ empty himself? Not of his divine nature. That was impossible. He continued to be the Son of God. ... Undoubtedly Christ gave up his environment of glory. He took upon himself limitations of place (space) and of knowledge and of power, though still on earth retaining more than any mere man" (Robertson, *Word Pictures*, 444).

47 "The text cannot mean that 'he *exchanged* the form of God for the form of a servant,' as is so often asserted. He took the form of servant while he retained the form of God!" (Hendriksen, *NTC*, 109). In my understanding, Paul does not describe an exchange (one for the other), but a contrast of the two natures: "the form of God" contrasted with "the form of a bond–servant." In becoming—and not merely pretending to be—a bond–servant, however, Jesus also chose not to exercise His divine privileges as God. There is no question that one nature had to be voluntarily subdued for the other nature to exist. As Lenski says, "Christ laid aside, emptied himself of the constant and plenary [complete—MY WORD] use of all that had been bestowed upon his human nature. If he had not done this he could not have wrought out our salvation. If he had come to earth only as his three disciples saw him on the Mount of Transfiguration, his redemptive obedience in his life, suffering, death, and resurrection, as the Gospels record it, would have been impossible" (*Interpretation*, 781).

Jesus not only assumed the form of a human bond–servant; He also subjected Himself to a human death, "even death on a cross" (2:8).[48] The cross was not just a painful, horrific, and torturous way to die; it was purposely designed to strip every shred of human dignity from the one being crucified. It was as if to advertise, "This person was not worthy to have ever lived!" In subjecting Himself to the cross, Jesus subjected Himself to a most demeaning, humiliating, and (for some) inexplicable death. The jeering, ridicule, and taunting contributed negatively to this awful experience, as did the beating with fists, pummeling with reeds, and contemptuous spittle of ungodly men (Mat. 27:27–30; see Isa. 50:6). Added to this were the crown of thorns and insinuations of being a false king and a false prophet ("Prophesy to us … !"—Mat. 26:68).

Then there was the scourging—a brutal whipping with leather straps embedded with bone or bits of metal—which was purposely designed to draw blood and lacerate the body (Mark 10:34, 15:15). Instead of the sanitized, effeminate–looking images of Jesus with small trickles of blood coming down from the crown of thorns (that artists have handed down to us), it is likely that Jesus was beaten and bloodied beyond recognition. After all this, He was forced to lay upon His flayed back while Roman soldiers mercilessly pounded rough metal spikes through His wrists and feet and into His cross, then erected this cross and set it into a hole in the ground. To cap off this wretched experience, Christ was crucified between two men who in fact *deserved* to die—two common criminals who represented the offenders of all of humanity (Luke 23:33). For six literally *excruciating* hours, Jesus hung upon the cross, His back and sides horribly lacerated, His face bruised and swollen, His body covered with blood, spittle, sweat, and dirt, His heart pounding, and His lungs gasping for breath.[49] This is not a nice, clean, sterilized picture of death; this is death in all of its unspeakable gruesomeness (Psalm 22:7–8, 13–18, and Isa. 52:14).

---

48   This was the great scandal (or, offense) that made it so difficult for many Jews to see Jesus as Messiah: to be hanged upon a tree is to be cursed of God (Deut. 21:23, Gal. 3:13). Yet it was necessary that Jesus come in the likeness of human flesh and die in likeness of one cursed of God to satisfy (or propitiate) the wrath of God that is otherwise directed toward us (Rom. 3:23–25, 5:9, and 8:3).

49   I say "literally *excruciating* hours" because "excruciate" means "(out) of the cross."

The Philippians are no doubt familiar with this scene. It is possible that retired soldiers who were members of the church in Philippi even participated in conducting a crucifixion. If not, then it is even more likely that these men have witnessed death by crucifixion, since this kind of execution is Rome's way of keeping law and order. Thus, Paul does not have to go into all the dreadful details of Jesus' death; they have seen this kind of death with their own eyes. (In contrast, most of us today probably would not have the stomach to witness an actual crucifixion.) Yet Paul does not focus only on the manner of Jesus' death, but more so the *injustice* of it. Being the Son of God, Jesus deserved to be honored and worshiped, never humiliated and tortured. He had committed no sin but was "obedient to the point of death"—He never committed a single crime and thus was not worthy of any punishment. Nonetheless, He died a truly innocent man, and His death became the most inhumane act and worst injustice that the world has ever seen: the Creation's murder of its own Creator.

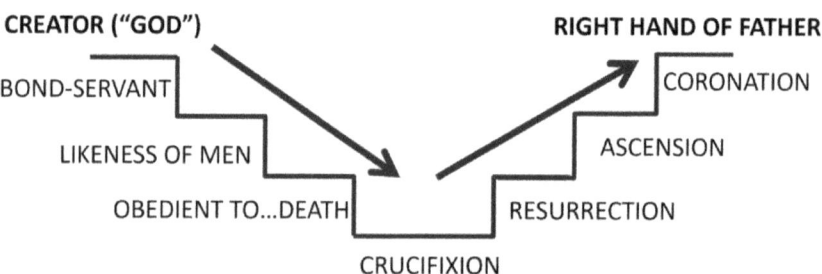

God Exalts His Son (2:9–11): Having descended into the very darkest, most pitiful experience of what it means to be "human," Jesus then ascended from that place through His resurrection (John 10:18). Having walked out of His own grave, God then highly exalted His Son for His obedience, worthiness, and self-sacrifice (2:9; see Isa. 52:13). The Lamb of God had been slain, but now He lives again by His own power! His blood had been shed to redeem countless souls, but He bleeds and suffers no more (Rev. 5:6–10). In His human state, Jesus was made "a little while lower than the angels" (Heb. 2:9), but He is no longer human (2 Cor. 5:16), He is no longer humiliated, and now He reigns over all of heaven. The Name of Jesus—referring to His position, authority, and divine nature—is no longer a name of alleged weakness or reproach, as it seemed to those who crucified Him, but is a name of power, glory, and salvation (Acts 4:12).[50]

"[A]t the name of Jesus every knee will bow" (2:10)—a quote lifted from Isa. 45:23 in reference to God Himself, which again makes Jesus an equal with God (as a divine Being). Paul refers to some future occasion, as in the Final Judgment, in which every authority that exists in heaven or on earth (Eph. 1:22–23, Col. 1:16) will profess submission and render homage to the King of kings and Lord of lords (2:11; see Rev. 19:16). Christ was a Servant to us to become our Redeemer, yet He is a Servant no more, but rules over all that has been created. "[T]o the glory of God the Father"—the ultimate purpose of Christ's servitude as well as His triumphant reign over the kingdom of God is to bring honor and praise to His Father. In due time, after the physical system has been ended and the opportunity for redemption has run its full course, Christ will hand the kingdom back to His Father and will be a Husband to His Bride (the church) for the eternity to come (1 Cor. 15:23–26, Rev. 19:7–9).

---

50 "The movement of the hymn [2:5–11] ought to be noticed. It has been from heaven (preexistence) to earth (incarnation) and finally to the underworld (death)" (Harrell, *TLWC*, 93)—and then a return to heaven (glorification).

Working Out One's Salvation (2:12–18)

Working Out One's Salvation (2:12–13): Returning to his earlier thought, Paul repeats his admonition to be faithful and obedient regardless of whether he comes to them soon (2:12; recall 1:27). "[W]ork out your salvation with fear and trembling" does *not* mean "Save yourselves by your own works," since Paul has taught elsewhere (e.g., Gal. 5:1–4) that human effort is unable to bring about spiritual salvation. Nonetheless, each believer is responsible to live obediently to the Lord since this is our "work" *as* believers. While grace is the divine power of our salvation, we are not saved *apart* from obedient faith (Eph. 2:8). This faith needs constant vigilance and regular maintenance (2 Peter 1:5–7). While one's salvation does have a beginning—a point in time when he is *saved* when before he had been *lost*—the full process of salvation requires continued faith. God is faithful to do His part; we must be faithful to do ours. Working out one's salvation requires a constant application of those things that make salvation real and anticipated.[51] Lipscomb provides this insight:

> To work out one's salvation is to comply with the conditions on which God has promised to save. To so live in accordance with God's words that he will be fitted to be saved. The thing for man to do is to fit himself for salvation, then God will save him. He can be fitted for salvation only by complying with the law God has given to discipline and fit him.[52]

Thus, the Philippians must obey Paul's apostolic authority, but in the end each believer personally answers to God. This warning also implies that one can *fail* to maintain his soul's integrity; otherwise, the "fear and trembling" aspect is meaningless. "Fear" can mean reverence or terror, depending on the context; in the present case, both meanings apply. We ought to have great reverence for God and recognize our smallness in comparison to His greatness (Heb. 12:28). At the same time, we ought

---
51 Hendriksen, *NTC*, 120.
52 Lipscomb, *Commentary*, 186.

to be afraid of the power that God possesses to *destroy* those who are disobedient to Him (Mat. 10:28). Thus, "fear" has to do with God as much as it does the difficulty of the task laid before us. "Trembling [lit., quaking with fear]"[53] implies a humble realization that no matter how hard we work, we are unable to do *all* that must be done. Despite our best efforts, we are still dependent upon the mercy and grace of God to compensate for our inadequacy.

Another reason to conduct oneself with "fear and trembling" is because "God … is at work in you" (2:13). It is an awesome and sobering realization to know that the God of heaven is directly intervening in one's life. No one can bring about his own salvation; only through the will of God actively working in one's life (and soul) can he be saved. It is not as though we are putting forth a little effort and God is doing far more; rather, it is that we are putting forward *all* our efforts and God is putting forth all *His* effort. Only when our will is in harmony with His, however, can the union of these two efforts—immensely unequal in performance, yet equal in necessity—bring about the perfect result. It is God's will and "good pleasure" that we are saved (1 Tim. 2:3–4).

The Believer's Responsibility (2:14–16): Perhaps *because* the Philippians have been doing so well, Paul needs to caution them against rivalries and competitions. "Grumbling" and "disputing" (2:14) may be the result of one person pitting his accomplishments against that of another, and the other person rebutting him. "It was popular among the Aristotelian philosophers around Philippi to impress others with their accomplishments; the Christians were not to take up this pastime."[54] Regardless of the specific reason for Paul's admonition here, it is good advice for all believers. Such displays of worldly behavior only give opponents of Christians reason to criticize them (Titus 2:6–8). Instead, believers are to be blameless of any legitimate accusations of wrongdoing and innocent of evil (2:15; see Rom. 16:19, 1 Cor. 14:40, and 1 Peter 2:12). "Children of God" must hold themselves to a far better and higher standard than that of sons of darkness (Eph. 5:7–13). Every generation

---

53   Strong, *Dictionary* (electronic), G5156.
54   JFB, *Commentary* (electronic), on 2:14.

of the unconverted is "crooked and perverse"; no generation is free from such moral blight.[55] It is our responsibility to provide "light" and "salt" to a lost and dying world (Mat. 5:13–16); we cannot do this if we imitate the world's selfish conduct. The "lights" here literally refers to cosmic luminaries—the sun, moon, and stars. Likewise, we are not merely to expose the deeds of darkness, but also to provide illumination for the *right* way in which to walk instead.

"[H]olding fast the word of life" (2:16) means to cling tenaciously to the gospel of Christ without letting go, but also holding it forth as a torch to light the path that leads to God. The word of God is a light to our own path (Psalm 119:105), but when we reflect this light, it becomes a source of illumination for others as well. "[S]o that ... I will have reason to glory"—i.e., Paul does not want to have his work among the Philippians to be in vain; he wants to give a favorable account of them when he stands before the Lord (cf. 1 Thess. 2:19–20). The "day of Christ" cannot mean anything in this context but the "day" when all men will stand before Him for judgment (Rom. 2:16, 2 Cor. 5:10). By implication, this thought also includes the second *appearance* of Christ (see comments on 1:6).

Paul's View of His Ministry (2:17–18): Yet, while Paul holds open the possibility that Christ will return in his own lifetime, he also holds open the possibility of his own execution (2:17). A "drink offering" (a.k.a. libation) alludes to the oil or wine that accompanied grain offerings prescribed by the Law of Moses (Lev. 2:1, 23:13, etc.). In one sense, Paul sees himself as an offering that is alongside (but not equal to) Christ's own offering (2 Tim. 4:6). In another sense, Paul considers his life as a type of accompanying sacrifice for the brethren at Philippi and elsewhere. This latter sense is supported by what follows—"the sacrifice and service of your faith"—as though the two ministries (Paul's and the Philippians') worked together for one grand sacrifice of service to God. (In this view, Paul considers himself as the smallest part of the

---

55 "Crooked" comes from the Greek *skolios*, from which we get the word "scoliosis" (i.e., a crookedness of the spine). "Perverse" [Greek, *diastrepho*] means to turn aside from the right path, or to corrupt or distort the truth (Thayer, *Lexicon* [electronic], G4646 and G1294).

offering, and the Philippians' work as the main offering.[56]) If Paul must die for the sake of fellow believers, then it will be a worthwhile and noble death. In anticipation of this possibility, Paul has reason to rejoice and communicate his joy with them, since this will be a fruitful and rewarding conclusion to his apostolic work. This joy is, of course, to be reciprocated by the Philippians in their appreciation for all that Paul has done for them (2:18).

---

56   Coffman, *Commentary*, 290.

The Coming of Timothy and Epaphroditus (Phil. 2:19–30)

While we know of no internal problems within the church at Philippi, certainly these Christians faced external pressure and persecution from the Jews (as in nearly every place that churches have been established). They may have also experienced residual fallout from the same craftsmen who had Paul and Silas arrested (see Acts 16:16ff). Thus, Paul plans to send two men, Timothy (2:19) and Epaphroditus (2:25), to give them encouragement while he himself remains in prison. The Philippians know of both men and have a good rapport with them. Timothy will be sent to observe the true nature of the church in Philippi and will send a report of their "condition" back to Paul—a report that Paul anticipates will be positive (2:19).

Paul's High Regard for Timothy (2:19–24): Paul often dispatched Timothy, one of his most trusted protégés, to various hot spots within the brotherhood, as an extension of Paul's own influence. Paul has a fatherly affection for Timothy, calling him his "true child in the faith" (1 Tim. 1:2) and his "beloved son" (2 Tim. 1:2). But here he gives his greatest compliment to this fine man: "For I have no one else of kindred spirit … " (2:20). The phrase "kindred spirit" comes from a single Greek word [*isopsuchos*] which means "like–minded."[57] In Paul's estimation, Timothy knows Paul better than any other man knows him, and he shares Paul's passion for the Lord and his love for the brethren. This makes him an ideal representative: sending Timothy to the Philippians is as close as possible to Paul being there in person. Timothy will be as "genuinely [or, naturally]" concerned for the church's welfare as Paul is. This disposition of Timothy's is contrasted with other brethren (who were with Paul at the time?) who sought their own interests, but not always the Lord's (2:21).[58] The Philippians had already seen Timothy's

---

57 Strong, *Dictionary* (electronic), G2473.

58 "Attempts have been made to tone down the sharpness of this judgment. This is hardly warranted. The words are simple and direct, whether read in the original or in translation. With many interpreters I believe, however, that they do not apply to absolutely every gospel-worker who was at this time in any way whatever associated with

character and his "proven worth" firsthand, so that Paul does not need to endorse him any further (2:22). In serving Paul, he is "like a child serving his father"—a fitting match, since Timothy's father is not a Christian (Acts 16:3) and Paul has no biological children. Paul plans to come to Philippi himself when he is released from prison, but at this point he is still waiting for a definite outcome to his circumstances (2:23–24).

Paul's Commendation of Epaphroditus (2:25–30): Meanwhile, Paul has also sent Epaphroditus—the assumed bearer of this epistle—because he also is a very capable man, and because of his personal interest in the situation at Philippi (2:25).[59] Paul calls Epaphroditus "my brother and fellow worker and fellow soldier"—a compliment of high praise, especially coming from a Christian soldier like Paul. Furthermore, he refers to him as "your messenger and minister to my need," indicating a man who is trustworthy and not afraid to serve.[60]

Epaphroditus had come *from* Philippi (at an indefinite time in the past), having delivered a gift from those Christians to Paul (see 4:18). Now, Paul is returning the favor by sending this valuable worker back to them for their spiritual encouragement. Likewise, Epaphroditus himself wants to go to Philippi, since the news of his personal illness has brought added distress to the Philippians and he wants them to know that he has recovered (2:26–27).[61] This must have been a severe sickness, one "to the point of death," but God spared him to continue his ministry

---

the apostle [as Luke or Aristarchus], but rather to those only who might be available at this particular juncture, and who might for a moment be regarded as qualified for a mission to Philippi" (Hendriksen, *NTC*, 135; bracketed words are mine).

59   His name "is a good, common, pagan name—one formed from the name of the Greek goddess Aphrodite" (Harrell, *TLWC*, 107).

60   The word "messenger" means "apostle" [Greek, *apostolos*], but clearly this word is used in a generic sense (as in Acts 14:4 [Barnabas and Paul] and 2 Cor. 8:23) rather than referring to the Christ-appointed apostolic office.

61   Once again, it is interesting to note that, while Paul had the power to heal, he did not use this power on his own fellow ministers. Thus, he did not heal Epaphroditus, and he left Trophimus sick in Miletus (2 Tim. 4:20). Our conclusion is: just as Jesus did not use His divine power for Himself (Mat. 4:1–4), so Paul did not use (or was not permitted to use) his miraculous healing for what might be considered selfish reasons.

to Paul and the churches. For this, Paul is thankful since the news of Epaphroditus' death would have dealt a strong blow to his own state of mind. "[S]orrow upon sorrow" indicates the sorrowfulness that Paul has already experienced as a prisoner—the only dark expression in this otherwise bright and optimistic epistle.

"Receive him … and hold men like him in high regard" (2:29)—a statement like what Paul has written elsewhere (1 Cor. 16:15–16 and 1 Thess. 5:12–13). Those who devote their lives in service to the Lord and His churches are worthy of honorable reception and high reputation. Particularly, those who put their own lives on the line for the brethren are to be commended for such self-sacrifice (Rom. 16:3–4, 2 Cor. 11:23–28, etc.). "Minister" (2:25) and "service" (2:30) come from the same Greek root word which indicates a priestly service or spiritual ministry.[62]

---

62 JFB, *Commentary* (electronic), on 2:30. Compare this with Rom. 12:1–2, where every Christian's service to God is characterized as a priestly ministry offering up gifts and sacrifices.

SECTION THREE:
THE HEAVENLY PERSPECTIVE (3:1–21)

Gaining Christ through the Sacrifice of All Things (Phil. 3:1–11)

"Finally" (3:1)—lit., "as to what remains"—is often used to indicate the closing of a letter. Paul may have *meant* to close the letter here originally, but then thought it necessary to add the following material (an entire chapter's worth!). He appears to pick up later (in 4:4) where he leaves off here.

An Encouragement and Warning (3:1–3): In any case, Paul's mind has clearly transitioned to different subjects than what he has just covered. His encouragement to "rejoice in the Lord" (3:1) is exceptional, coming from a man imprisoned for two years. The cause for or source of this rejoicing has nothing to do with his circumstances, however, but is "in the Lord." Many people in world rejoice over things that are not of God (e.g., Rom. 1:32 and Rev. 11:10); yet Christians alone are able to rejoice "in the Lord" over whatever will advance the cause of Christ. Rejoicing, then, is a personal expression of gratitude and satisfaction for one's participation in the work of God. Likewise, "joy" is second among Paul's description of the "fruit of the Spirit" (Gal. 5:22–23), indicating its importance and relevance in the Christian's walk *with* the Spirit. This is not the first time in the present epistle that Paul has focused on "joy" or "rejoicing" (recall 1:25); yet he sees no difficulty in the healthy repetition of this thought.

"Beware of the dogs … " (3:2–3)—this is Paul's assessment of those Jews who pride themselves on their heritage, conformity to the Law of Moses, and controlling interest over Gentile converts (Gal. 6:12–13). People in the ancient world did not regard dogs as household pets as they do today, but as useless and expendable scavengers. They often roamed through the countryside in packs as wild animals (like jackals or dingoes). A live dog represented a low form of life (Eccles. 9:4); a dead dog represented something which deserved no recognition of loss since it was considered an insignificant creature to begin with (1 Sam. 17:43). The Jews habitually regarded Gentiles as dogs (Mat. 15:26) or worthless people; those who disregard the gospel of Christ make themselves out to be dogs and swine (Mat. 7:6, Rev. 22:15). In a sad reversal of fortune, Jews who reject the gospel (which many Gentiles have readily received) become "dogs" instead, having repudiated the message that came from heaven (Acts 13:46).

In the present passage (3:2–3), "dogs," "evil workers," and "the false circumcision" all refer to the same people: Jewish teachers who either wholly reject the gospel of Christ or malign it with their imposed teachings of Law, rituals (like circumcision), and justification by works. Such men consider themselves to be pious and righteous to God, yet Jesus calls them "a synagogue of Satan" (Rev. 2:9; cf. John 8:44–47). "False circumcision" refers to a circumcision that really does not accomplish anything.[63] The "{true} circumcision" refers to an action that Christ performs upon the human heart—i.e., the removal of the condemnation of God (Col. 2:11–12)—thus, transformation of the heart versus cutting of the flesh. (There is no "true" in the original text.) Physical circumcision no longer has any spiritual significance; it no longer serves as a sign of a covenant relationship between men and God (as before; see Gen. 17:10–11). Spiritual circumcision is a matter of the heart, not the human body; one's confidence is no longer on what he does in the flesh, but what Christ does for him (Rom. 2:28–29). Only such people can "worship in the Spirit of God" because they seek to worship Him in spirit and truth (John 4:23–24) rather than seeking to justify themselves through physical works.

---

63 The word [Greek, *katatome*] translated "false circumcision" means "concision" or "mutilation"; it is not the typical word used for ritual circumcision (Thayer, *Lexicon* [electronic], G2699). "Concision refers to flesh-cutting rituals, which carried connotations of disgrace and disapproval. Though necessary for all people under the old covenant, circumcision became more and more associated in the apostle's experience with the open hostility of the NT Jews and with the warped teachings of the false brethren" (JFB, *Commentary* [electronic], on 3:2).

Paul Recalls His Past (3:4–6): Even though Paul has just warned not to put any confidence "in the flesh," he draws upon his own personal experience as a rising star in the Jewish world as being far more sincere and impressive than these other Jews (i.e., "dogs") who flaunt their own heritage and status (3:4; cf. 2 Cor. 11:21–28). Paul's point is not to boast, but quite the contrary: he intends to show how hopeless it is to put confidence in human achievement as a means of self-justification. It is as if to say, "If anyone ought to boast, it should be me—yet all that I once relied upon is useless in comparison to what I have gained in Christ." Nonetheless, for the sake of argument, Paul lays out his credentials (3:5–6):

- ❑ "circumcised the eighth day"—i.e., a valid, covenant-bound member of the nation of Israel, according to the Law of Moses (Lev. 12:3). Paul's point here is to demonstrate his (former) loyalty to the covenant and the Law, to rebuff accusations that he was a traitor to these. In fact, by accepting Christ as Israel's Redeemer, Paul was more loyal than those who accused him of selling out (see Acts 24:14–15 and 28:23).
- ❑ "of the nation of Israel"—i.e., not a proselyte, but a full-fledged, pure-blooded Jew. Paul was the genuine article and not a Johnny-come-lately who joined the Jewish nation and tried to ride on the coattails of its heritage.
- ❑ "of the tribe of Benjamin"—Paul is able to trace his lineage all the way back to one of the founding patriarchs of the nation of Israel. Thus, his connection to Israel is not based on his opinion but is substantiated by genealogical records.
- ❑ "a Hebrew of Hebrews"—i.e., not a Hellenist (i.e., a Greek-cultured Jew), but one immersed in Hebrew law, customs, and religion since his youth. This does not mean he has not been educated in secular history, but that he has always stringently maintained the purity of his ancient roots (Acts 22:3).[64]

---

64 "The grounds of boasting so far has been threefold. He had made the claim of ritual purity (circumcised according to the Law); racial purity (Israelite of the tribe of Benjamin); and now cultural purity (of a Hebrew family)" (Harrell, *TLWC*, 117).

- "as to the Law, a Pharisee"—referring to one of the strictest sects among the Jews. The party of the Pharisees originated during the post-exilic (and intertestamental) period as Jews struggled to maintain the purity and enforcement of the Law against an incoming tide of Greek (Hellenistic) culture, philosophies, and secular influences. "Pharisee" is believed to have come from a word meaning "separate." Accordingly, they separated themselves from the common Jews, whom many Pharisees believed were ignorant of the Law and its meaning (John 7:49).[65] Paul states, then, that he is the son of a Pharisee, was a devout Pharisee himself, and was fully committed to that sect's beliefs (Acts 23:6). His view (or interpretation) of the Law thus followed exactly this belief system.

- "as to zeal, a persecutor of the church"—i.e., his zeal for defending the Law (as a Pharisee) necessarily led him to silence all those who, in his own mind, violated the Law in order to pursue their blasphemous religion. He was not passive in this defense, but aggressive (see Acts 26:9–11 for his own graphic depiction of this). In another place, he admitted that he "persecuted this Way [i.e., the gospel] to the death, binding and putting both men and women into prisons … " (Acts 22:4; cf. Acts 9:1–3). In this respect, Paul virtually single-handedly instigated an area-wide persecution against the church, which was far more than any of his contemporaries had done.

- "as to righteousness … , found blameless"—i.e., regarding ceremonial and legal righteousness. If any person were to scrutinize Paul's pre–Christian life, he would see that he was a man who meticulously, piously, and fervently obeyed the Law's smallest details. Like many Jewish teachers, Paul sought righteousness through law-keeping rather than through grace (Rom. 10:2–4), yet at the time did not realize his huge mistake.

Such is the character sketch of a man who justified himself before God, and who defended His honor and His laws more tenaciously than all others. Paul was not an outwardly arrogant man, but in his pre–converted state of mind he did place full confidence "in the flesh,"

---

65 Lenski, *Interpretation*, 834.

seeking to be justified by his status and credentials rather than by the grace of God.

Counting All Things as Loss for Christ (3:7–11): "But … I have counted [those things] as loss for the sake of Christ" (3:7). This statement marks the crucial turning point in Paul's thinking as well as his life. Indeed, the church and the entire world have never been the same since this great conversion. Though blinded temporarily on the road to Damascus (Acts 9:1–16), his spiritual sight became clearer than ever. He could now see that to which his self-righteousness had previously blinded him. All that he so strenuously pursued through Jewish pride and law-keeping suddenly paled in comparison to what he had discovered in Christ. To count something as "loss" here means to regard it as valueless *in comparison to* or *in exchange for* something else. Thus, Paul's Israelite parentage, Jewish heritage, Pharisaic training, etc. simply could not do for him what Christ alone could do.

"More than that," he continues, "I count all things to be loss … " (3:8)—i.e., not only things pertaining to his religion, but he counted *all* things in *whatever* context as "loss."[66] We must keep in mind that Paul is making *comparative* statements ("This is better than that") rather than *evaluative* statements ("This is worthless; that alone is valuable"). His Jewish upbringing, rabbinic training, life experiences, etc. did not suddenly become valueless since he draws upon these heavily in his apostolic ministry. However, they cannot accomplish for him what he hoped they would do. In comparison to Christ, they are "rubbish" [lit., dung or refuse]; thus, Christ is *worth* the "loss of all things." All of Paul's earthly status and accomplishments (as an Israelite, as a Pharisee, etc.) cannot overcome his sinful disposition before God; despite all his previous efforts, he remained a condemned sinner. Christ, however, changed everything: now he can serve God with a clear conscience and in genuine righteousness.

---

66 "He has not, indeed, informed us of the exact extent of his loss in becoming a Christian. It is by no means improbable that he had been excommunicated by the Jews; and that he had been disowned by his own family" (Barnes, *Barnes' Notes*, 195).

To "gain Christ" does not merely mean "to be a Christian." It is not merely a change of status (from "sinner" to "Christian") but also implies the establishment of a new relationship with God based upon the intercession of Christ. This more accurately defines "knowing Christ Jesus my Lord" (3:9)—Paul personally identifies *with* Him rather than merely having a fact-based knowledge *of* Him. Likewise, to "be found in Him" (3:10) means to have fellowship with Him and enjoy all the privileges of that fellowship (up to and including salvation itself). "[N]ot having a righteousness of my own … but that which is through faith in Christ"—i.e., not trying to obtain righteousness through works (of law) but in demonstrations of his faith in Christ (Rom. 1:17). The change of heart from a strict, self-righteous Pharisee to an obedient Christian that sought justification by grace was immediate; the fruits of this change would manifest themselves over time.[67] Paul then summarizes the broader scope of this fellowship (3:10–11):

- "that I may know Him"—personally, experientially, and in a life-transforming manner. This knowledge translates into (or, is reciprocated by) a "walk" that is consistent with the One whom he knows (recall 1:27).
- "and the power of His resurrection"—the power to raise Jesus from the dead is the same power (and comes from the same Source) that justifies the sinner before God. Thus, Paul has confidence that God *can* pronounce him "righteous" because of the power and authority He has already manifested in Jesus' resurrection (Eph. 1:18–20, 1 Peter 1:3–5, 3:21–22, etc.).
- "and the fellowship [or, sharing] in His sufferings"—i.e., any suffering for His sake and the sake of righteousness (Mat. 5:10–12) that He expects of those who identify with Him (Rom. 8:16–17). Barnes says this:

> Many are willing to reign with Christ, but they would not be willing to suffer with him; many would be willing to wear a crown of glory like him, but not the crown of thorns; many would be willing to put on the robes

---

67 JFB, *Commentary* (electronic), on 3:9.

of splendor which will be worn in heaven, but not the scarlet robe of contempt and mockery. They would desire to share the glories and triumphs of redemption, but not its poverty, contempt, and persecution. This was not the feeling of Paul. He wished in all things to be *just like Christ*, and hence he counted it an honor to be permitted to suffer as he did.[68]

- "being conformed to His death"—not, "equating my experiences of suffering with His," but, "suffering for the same cause—to do the will of God—as exemplified and epitomized in Christ's own death." Paul "conformed" to Christ's death in his baptism (Rom. 6:3–7), but he continues to conform to that death every time he suffers personal loss and puts to death the will of the flesh for the Lord's sake.
- "that I may attain to the resurrection from the dead"—or, in the present context, "that I myself may participate in (the) resurrection, just as Jesus did." Paul clearly understands that *all* believers will experience a physical resurrection from the dead in the likeness of Christ's own physical resurrection (Rom. 6:5, 1 Cor. 15:21–23, 1 Thess. 4:13–17, etc.). Thus, "knowing Christ" naturally leads to a realistic expectation of this resurrection, which will be shared with all those who have been made "worthy" to participate in it (see Luke 20:35). "Knowing Christ" is commensurate with salvation *in* Christ, since to "know" Him leads to one's real and visible salvation (1 John 2:3–4).

---

68 Barnes, *Barnes' Notes*, 197.

Letting Go to Move Forward
(Phil. 3:12–21)

Paul has just outlined his objectives: seeing the power of Christ's resurrection, fully understanding the fellowship of His sufferings, etc. Taken out of context, his words might sound overconfident and boastful, but such a conclusion would be incorrect. He clarifies himself in the following verses. "Not that I have already obtained {it}" (3:12)—"it" is necessarily implied, but refers to all the things he had just mentioned. These things Paul pursues, and he has left everything else behind to pursue them, but he is a work in progress and has not yet "become perfect" in every sense. "[B]ut I press on so that … "—in essence, "I keep striving to obtain the very thing which Christ made possible for me to obtain." This does not contradict what he said earlier (about not seeking a righteousness of his own—recall 3:9) but emphasizes his own part in this process of being perfected. God does not perfect His saints *apart* from their own effort, but they must fully cooperate *with* Him to this end.

Pressing Forward in Christ (3:13–16): While perfection in Christ is Paul's goal, he remains realistic and practical about how this happens. He will not be saved by an epiphany or mere confidence alone, but through a process of letting go of what hinders him to pursue what will be in his best interest. Thus, "I do not regard myself as having laid hold of it yet"—a restatement of what he just said (in 3:12), yet with renewed emphasis. "His line of argument [now] becomes: I was a better Jew than they [i.e., my contemporaries] but I do not claim to be as good a Christian."[69] "[F]orgetting what lies behind and reaching forward to what lies ahead" (3:13) provides a God–given strategy for spiritual maturity. Unfortunately, some Christians may not follow this apostolic instruction. Instead, they try in vain to "reach forward" while *not* forgetting "what lies behind." In other words, they may:

❑ choose to be obsessed with their poor decisions or personal failures of the past.

---
69 Harrell, *TLWC*, 123; bracketed words are mine.

- allow hurts, offenses, and injustices of the past rob them of joy in the Lord.
- allow the damaging words of people in their past to discourage their hope for the future.
- blame others for "why I can't be more spiritual" or "why I can't draw near to God."
- be unwilling to forgive their offenders (or at least cultivate a Christ-like heart *of* forgiveness—Col. 3:12–15).
- cling to brooding anger, bitterness, resentment, and even cynicism as a means of coping with all the wrongs that have been committed against them.
- resign themselves to a "that's just that way I am" disposition—and thus ruin any opportunity for positive change, personal growth, or spiritual maturity.
- refuse to let go of sinful behavior, addictions, and attitudes.
- choose to remain in a pattern of self-destruction and self-limitation.
- make excuses for their *lack* of growth rather than do what it takes to *grow*.
- refuse to "add" to their faith (2 Peter 1:5–7) and then are disappointed when their faith remains small and unproductive.
- be unwilling to believe in the power of the gospel (Rom. 1:16, 1 Cor. 1:18) and its life-transforming message.
- be unwilling to believe in the willingness and/or ability of Christ to overcome their seemingly insurmountable obstacles to salvation.
- refuse to study God's word (2 Tim. 2:15).
- refuse to be devoted to prayer (Col. 4:2).
- refuse to participate in the assemblies of the saints (Heb. 10:24–25).
- try to outsmart God by doing what He said *not* to do but hoping they will be successful anyway (e.g., Mat. 6:24).
- try to hold onto this world while claiming to seek the things above (Col. 3:1–3, 1 John 2:15–17).
- be unwilling to let go of religious or family traditions to embrace "sound doctrine" (or, erroneously think these traditions are *on par with* sound doctrine).
- resist the guidance of the Holy Spirit (Gal. 5:16–17).
- refuse to do the will of the Father (Mat. 7:21).

The point is: no one can "reach forward" who will not first let go of what keeps him from reaching forward. The logic is simple; emotional interference and one's own unbelief are what complicate things. We cannot think that sin does not exist, or that we have not (even recently) fallen victim to it. At the same time, we also cannot think we are drawing near to God while our heart remains anchored to this fallible life. To "forget" what lies behind does not mean we pretend that the past did not really happen. It means to dwell upon that past no longer; refuse to allow it to dictate the future; refuse to obsess over it at the expense of one's future life with God. "Let us not spend our time either in pondering the gloomy past, and our own unfaithfulness, or in thinking of what we have done, and thus becoming puffed up with self-complacency; but let us keep the eye steadily on the prize, and run the race as though we had just commenced it."[70]

Once we let go of what lies behind us, then we can successfully pursue—by the grace of God—what lies before us. "I press on toward the goal … " (3:14)—the implication is that of an athlete giving everything to win the race, straining forward to cross the finish line, looking to the prize ("the crown of righteousness"—2 Tim. 4:8). This is an "upward call" because it leads the believer heavenward and does not allow him to remain fixed upon the things here below (see Col. 3:1–3). This "call" is "of God in Christ Jesus"—i.e., God has called us with a heavenly calling (Heb. 3:1) through His Son's ministry of reconciliation (2 Cor. 5:18–21). Thus, "as many as are perfect [or, mature]" will have this attitude of forgetting what lies behind and pressing forward to the upward call (3:15). This instruction is for all believers, not only the Philippians. It compares the mature in Christ to those with far less maturity; thus, "perfect" in this context is relative, not objective.[71] To paraphrase 3:15b: "If your attitude is different than what I have just described, in time God will disclose to you this error (and you will be expected to correct that) [implied]." Even so, we are to live according to what we *presently* know to be true until Scripture reveals otherwise. For this reason, "[L]et us keep living by that same standard to which we have [thus far] attained" (3:16,

---

70 Barnes, *Barnes' Notes*, 201.
71 Lipscomb, *Commentary*, 209.

bracketed words added). This standard (or rule) is the same as what Paul taught in all the churches (1 Cor. 4:17).

The Need to Follow the Pattern (3:17–19): Paul does not just tell others what to think or how to live, but he practices what he preaches. Several times in his epistles he puts himself up as an example for others to follow (1 Cor. 4:16, 11:1, 2 Thess. 3:7–9, etc.): "Brethren, join in following my example … " (3:17). He instructs these Christians to "observe those who walk according to the pattern" that Christ has revealed to Paul. This "according to the pattern" concept has its roots in the Law, where God told Moses to follow the explicit pattern He gave to him concerning the construction of the tabernacle (Exod. 25:9, 40; see Acts 7:44 and Heb. 8:5). The pattern for one's Christian life is far more important than that of a primitive tent of worship; our "temple" is a living thing, not a lifeless structure (1 Cor. 6:19–20). Likewise, the entire spiritual body of Christ is a living organism ("a holy temple in the Lord") that is built according to a specific heavenly pattern (Eph. 2:19–22).[72]

Not everyone who claims to be "of God" walks according to this pattern, however. Those who refuse to comply with this heavenly pattern "are enemies of the cross of Christ" (3:18), since no one can walk contrary to Christ and still be a friend of God (Mat. 12:30, James 4:4). Instead of reaching forward to the upward call of God in Christ, such people fixate on things of this world, which includes their human pride and self-sufficiency (as what we see in the Judaists who preach Christ but trust in "the flesh," as discussed earlier). Their end will be "destruction"—the self-inflicted ruin of their soul—because they resist the word of the cross (1 Cor. 1:18ff). Paul adds a brief but potent threefold description of such people (3:19):

- ❑ First, their god is not God the Father but their own "appetite [or, belly]." This refers to things that are of this life, temporary in nature,

---

[72] On this subject, I strongly recommend my book, *The New Testament Pattern: God's Plan for Christians and Their Churches* (Spiritbuilding Publishers, 2023); go to www.spiritbuilding.com/chad.

and destined for destruction (Rom. 6:13, 1 John 2:15–17). These are base and dishonorable "animal passions."[73]
- Second, they glory in that which is shameful, having repeatedly perverted what is good and honorable (Isa. 5:20). Lack of shame reveals a calloused conscience that no longer discerns between right and wrong: it has been violated so many times that it has lost all moral sensation.
- Third, they "set their minds on earthly things"—and thus they have their reward in full, however small and pathetic it is (cf. Mat. 6:1–2, 5).

Citizenship in Heaven (3:20–21): In sharp contrast, Christians who follow the God-given pattern are no longer citizens of this world, but "our citizenship [or, commonwealth] is in heaven" (3:20).[74] This likely has some allusion to Roman citizenship, which is regarded highly in Paul's day, and especially within a Roman city such as Philippi. Yet, those who walk in a manner worthy of the gospel of Christ (recall 1:27) have a far better and more valuable citizenship than anything than Rome or even this world can offer. To be a citizen of heaven (or sons of the kingdom—Mat. 13:38) indicates one's favorable standing with God and anticipates an eternal fellowship with Him. No wonder, then, that those who have this priceless citizenship "eagerly wait for a Savior" whose return will be to take them home to this heavenly glory (2 Peter 3:11–12, Heb. 9:27–28). When He appears, Christ will "transform" the physical bodies of believers into a glorified state that is in conformity with His own (3:21; see 1 John 3:2).

This brief description leaves questions unanswered, but it is not meant to be comprehensive or even explanatory. It only intends to bring the

---

73 Lipscomb, *Commentary*, 214.

74 "The word translated 'commonwealth' (*politeuma*) is interesting. As a verb (cf. 1:27) it meant the 'conduct of a citizen' or the 'behavior of any member of a group.' As a noun in this context it undoubtedly is correctly rendered 'commonwealth.' The apostle's point is not simply that he and others in Philippi were citizens of heaven. This could be equally claimed by the false teachers. The crux is the location of that 'commonwealth.' The opponents said it was already on earth: the end had been realized. Paul, in contrast, says it 'is in heaven': it is not present; it is future" (Harrell, *TLWC*, 129).

discussion full circle: while Christ has endured suffering and humiliation as a means of achieving glory, so we also must endure the fellowship of His sufferings (recall 3:10) before entering a glorified state of existence. Paul does not say anything (in the present text) about the resurrection of the righteous or the wicked (cf. John 5:28–29) but only to those who are alive at His coming: such people will be transformed and thus prepared for a glorified existence (see 1 Cor. 15:50–53). It is clear, however, that this transformation must also be made possible for those who have already died and will be bodily resurrected, especially since some believers had died in the Lord even during Paul's own lifetime (1 Cor. 15:6, 1 Thess. 4:13–14).

Yet how will Christ do this? How will He *raise* a body that has so decomposed that it is *no longer* a body? Our immediate answer is: If God can fashion dust into a pristine human being (as in Adam's case), then He most certainly can *re*-fashion our "dust" into a new living being. "If he [Christ] can subject *even all things*, the totality of all the powers of the universe, unto himself … , will he not be able to refashion our lowly body so that it will have a form like his own glorious body?"[75] The point is: we tend to focus on logistics, technical details, and natural processes, when all we are *told* to focus on is a belief in an all-powerful and all-knowing God with whom "all things are possible" (Mat. 19:26).

---

75 Hendriksen, *NTC*, 185; emphasis is his, bracketed word is mine.

Section Four: Reliance upon God (4:1–23)

Dwelling upon Excellence (4:1–9)

Paul's use of "beloved brethren" (4:1) again emphasizes his deep affection for the Christians in Philippi (recall 2:12). The fact that he uses this phrase twice in one sentence only further underscores this. Calling them his "joy and crown" is like what he says to those at Thessalonica (1 Thess. 2:19–20): indeed, he would say this of *all* genuine believers who followed his teaching and supported his ministry. At Christ's coming, whenever it happens, Paul hopes to hold the Philippians up as one of the excellent highlights of his ministry. His repeated admonition to "stand firm" (recall 1:27) is a standard theme in all his epistles.

A Call for Peace between Two Believers (4:2–3): "I urge Euodia and … Syntyche … " (4:2–3)—this is a (rare) personal appeal to two women (deaconesses?) who have been of great assistance to Paul's ministry, but now apparently are at odds with each other. Lenski notes, "This is not an unusual occurrence when energetic personalities are engaged in the same cause. [Yet] it was not a good thing for these two to differ as they did."[76] We do not know the reason for the disagreement, only that they are to work it out "in harmony in the Lord." "True companion" [NASB] or "true yokefellow" [KJV] comes from the Greek *suzugos* and is thought by some commentators to refer to an actual person ("loyal Syzygus"); others believe it refers to Timothy, Silas, or an elder of that church.[77] It is difficult to draw any firm conclusions from the text, and we may never know the actual meaning of the reference.

---

76 Lenski, *Interpretation*, 867; bracketed word is mine.

77 JFB, *Commentary* (electronic), on 4:2–3. Lenski, however, offers a lengthy explanation in support of this simply being a man's name (*Interpretation*, 868–74). Despite his defense, this does not seem to be a natural understanding of this word in this context. Regardless, the Bible student will have to come to his or her own conclusion on this matter.

In any case, Paul urges this "companion" to help these two women to reconcile their differences and return to the work of the Lord. He also asks this companion to help "Clement and the rest of my fellow workers" there in Philippi, though we do not know of these people other than what Paul mentions here. According to Origen, an early church writer, this Clement is the same man who became the bishop of Rome after the death of Peter and Paul, but this cannot be substantiated otherwise.[78] "[W]hose names are written in the book of life"—a reference to God's record of the faithful (see Luke 10:20, Rev. 20:12, and 21:27). In the ancient world, Roman "free" cities had a roster that contained all the names of those who resided there and thus had a right to citizenship. Here, Paul speaks of a much greater roster (or book; recording) of those who have citizenship within the kingdom of God, since "the Lord knows who are His" (2 Tim. 2:19).

Rejoice, Pray, and Find Peace (4:4–7): Earlier in the epistle, Paul wrote, "Finally, my brothers, rejoice in the Lord" (3:1). Now he resumes that thought and expounds upon it: "Rejoice in the Lord always; again I will say, rejoice" (4:4). Joy and rejoicing are obviously major themes of this epistle, and ought to be major themes of the Christian life. "Let your gentle {spirit} be known to all men" (4:5)—the word for "gentle" can be translated here "moderation," "forbearance," or "big-heartedness."[79] These all refer to the same kind of "spirit"—a word not in the text, but necessarily implied—i.e., one who lives in a Christ-like manner among believers and non-believers alike ("all men").

What motivates this behavior is the fact that "The Lord is near." This can refer to the nearness (in time) of Christ's actual appearance (recall 3:20–21); or, figuratively, it can mean that the Lord's presence is always among believers, and He sees all things (as in Mat. 18:20 or Heb. 4:12). The first meaning is the most natural, but then creates an alleged problem among believers: if Paul said that "the Lord is near," and yet 2,000 years have passed, how are we to believe in his credibility? Here is a proposed

---

78 JFB, on 4:3. Robertson says that there is "no evidence" for this (*Word Pictures*, 459), yet Coffman is convinced to the contrary (*Commentary*, 318).

79 Robertson, *Word Pictures*, 459.

response:
- Jesus made it clear—and Paul underscored this (1 Thess. 5:1–2)—that God has not revealed to us the "times or epochs" that pertain to the future, except in the most general sense (Acts 1:7). We know that Christ will come again; we do not know in what age, year, day, or hour He will come.
- Jesus, as a Son of Man (in the flesh), did not know the day or hour that Jerusalem would be destroyed (Mat. 24:36). Given this, it is not surprising that Paul does not know exactly when the Lord will return in glory—but he is free to offer his perspective.
- Based upon what they assumed intuitively (but not by inspiration), it seems that Paul, Peter, and John all believed that Jesus might come soon (compare Phil. 4:5 and 1 Peter 4:7 and 1 John 2:28).
- However, in 2 Thess. 2:1ff, Paul provides some events (or conditions) that must be fulfilled before the Lord can come. This bears upon Paul's use of "near": Jesus will not appear until these things have been fulfilled, but He could appear any time after that. Thus, Paul does not mean "near" as in "at any moment," but "His coming is not indefinitely prolonged." (Keep in mind, too, that Paul wrote *Thessalonians* years before he wrote *Philippians*.)
- Technically-speaking, the Lord *is* "near"—i.e., since we do not know when He will come, His coming is *always* "near." This creates a perpetual anticipation among believers who wait for their visual redemption (1 Thess. 5:4–6).

All said, we must take Paul's words in the context of what he was able to know rather than using them to pinpoint a definite time in history when Jesus would come. One thing is clear: when Jesus *does* come, it will be unmistakably evident, and will usher in the end of the physical system (2 Thess. 1:6–9, 2 Peter 3:3–10, and Rev. 1:7).[80]

---

[80] The doctrine of "realized eschatology" maintains that Jesus "appeared" in AD 70 in a "spiritual" sense, and that the resurrection (of "old covenant believers") has already taken place. Yet the NT simply does not teach this. It is true that Jesus came in judgment against Jerusalem (Israel) in AD 70; there is no contesting this. Yet, the NT speaks of three different "comings" of Christ: His judgment against Israel (as just mentioned); His judgment against the Roman Empire, which will include individual churches that refuse to repent (as in the letters to the seven churches in Rev. 2—3); and His judgment against the world, before which He will rescue His faithful and bring them into

"Be anxious for nothing ... " (4:6)—or, "Do not be troubled with cares or your thoughts," which is a common problem among all people. Jesus addressed this same thing and gave the same antidote as Paul: turn everything over to God (Mat. 6:25–34). "Prayer" is a general term; "supplication" implies calling upon God to *supply* something. In the exercise of prayer, the believer is to leave his anxious fears and concerns with the Lord and make requests of Him ("because He cares for you"—1 Peter 5:6–7). All such requests are to be "with thanksgiving," because God deserves our gratitude, and we do not deserve His kindness. This does not mean that we should only thank Him for things that seem beneficial to us, but we should thank Him for "everything." Hendriksen says, "Prayer without thanksgiving is like a bird without wings: such a prayer cannot rise to heaven, can find no acceptance with God."[81] We are to believe that God causes *all* things to work together for good, whether something seems "good" to us initially or not (Rom. 8:28). Our prayers are not to inform God of anything since He already knows all things (Mat. 6:8). Rather, prayer is an act of faith and a testing of our confidence in His ability to act. In place of our anxious thoughts and apprehensions, God responds with peace "which surpasses all comprehension [lit., the human mind]" (4:7)—i.e., a heavenly, soul-calming, unfathomable assurance that God is in control and will not abandon the one who looks to Him in faith (Heb. 11:6, 13:5–6). This calm assurance is available only for those "in Christ Jesus"; God will only guard the heart and mind of those in fellowship with Him.

Thinking on and Practicing Excellence (4:8–9): "Finally, brethren ... " (4:8)—the following prescription is the antidote for fear, worry, anxious thoughts, and the dread of one's circumstances. It also cultivates a cheerful outlook that looks beyond this unstable and fickle world and trusts instead in the stability and certainty of God's world. The "whatever" of this verse includes all things that fit the description of its counterpart. Thus, the things upon which we are to fix our attention

---

glory. All these comings share overlapping features, but they are hardly interchangeable, and those who lump them all into one "coming" do great harm to Christians' understanding of this important subject.

81 Hendriksen, *NTC*, 196.

include "whatever" is:

- "true"—truth is what God reveals to men and is the foundation of the Christian's belief in God (John 4:24). It is also the basis for spiritual freedom (John 8:31–32) and the certainty of one's heavenly future.
- "honorable"—lit., venerated for its character; dignified; upstanding.[82]
- "right"—in essence, "righteousness," or that which exactly conforms to God's holy nature. Whatever is "right" with God will be beneficial to the human soul; the person who is "right" with God will have nothing to fear in the age to come.
- "pure"—blameless, innocent, and free from moral corruption.
- "lovely"—acceptable, pleasing, or welcome (to God); lit., "friendly toward."[83]
- "of good repute"—or, that which is well-spoken of; words befitting a child of God (as opposed to the gutter language or profanity of worldly people—Eph. 5:3–5).
- "excellence"—or virtue (same word as in 1 Peter 2:9 and 2 Peter 1:3, 5). In classical Greek literature, this referred to manliness, moral courage to do what is right (regardless of the consequences), or moral goodness of any kind.[84] NT writers have taken this thought to its highest level in defining it as a divine attribute which we are to imitate.
- "worthy of praise"—lit., exemplary, commendable, or approved (by God).

These are the things upon which the believer is to set his mind, and which will thus govern his good behavior. "Dwell" here means to meditate heavily; take seriously into account; make a reckoning of (with the purpose of drawing conclusions).[85] In another sense, we might think of ruminating upon these things (like a cow chewing its cud) <u>thoughtfully, quietly, and unhurriedly.</u>

82 Strong, *Dictionary* (electronic), G4586.
83 Ibid., G4375.
84 Robertson, *Word Pictures*, 460.
85 Thayer, *Lexicon* (electronic), G3049.

The believer is not merely to dwell upon good thoughts, however; he is also to put into practice those things upon which he has given such serious attention (4:9). Christ's church cannot be filled with people who merely think good thoughts; He needs those people to be active servants and living witnesses as well. On the other hand, good behavior begins in the heart. "We grow like our thoughts; we cannot entertain impure thoughts without becoming corrupt, and we cannot think good thoughts without becoming pure. Meditation precedes, and works follow."[86] Once again, Paul offers himself as a model example of how he intends for the Philippians to conduct themselves (recall 3:17). After all, "The preacher is the interpreter of the spiritual life and should be an example of it."[87]

---

86 Lipscomb, *Commentary*, 226.
87 Robertson, *Word Pictures*, 460.

The Philippians' Support of Paul
(Phil. 4:10–19)

The Secret of Contentment (4:10–13): Paul abruptly changes the subject here as he winds up this epistle (4:10). The Philippians had supported Paul at an earlier time, but then "lacked opportunity" to do so for a while after this. Now, they have revived or refreshed their resolve to give him financial assistance, which is the underlying meaning of their "concern." "Not that I speak from want," Paul clarifies (4:11), since he has learned how to be content in all circumstances. "Content" here literally means self-sufficient; possessing enough to require no aid or support; independent of external circumstances.[88]

Obviously, Paul's self-sufficiency refers to physical needs, not spiritual. Instead of trying to protect an earthly lifestyle to which he had become accustomed (which is what many Christians do), he instead has learned to adapt to whatever situation in which he finds himself. His "I have learned" statement indicates that contentment is indeed a *learned* perspective, not a natural one (see 1 Tim. 6:6–8). In other words, Paul looks forward to the Philippians' help, but he can also survive without it. In the next verse (4:12), he briefly expounds on this thought. Whether destitution or prosperity, having enough to eat or going hungry, or having abundance or suffering need, "I have learned the secret" of how to find contentment in all circumstances. Again, "I have learned" indicates a perspective acquired over time, maturity, and experience.

"I can do all things through Him [i.e., Christ] who strengthens me" (4:13) means, "Whatever God needs me to do, Christ is the source of my strength for doing it" (Eph. 3:20, Col. 1:29). Sadly, this verse has been lifted out of context, misinterpreted, or simply misunderstood by many believers and pseudo-believers alike. Many think this means, "Whatever I want to do for God, Christ will 'strengthen' me to do it!" This view justifies any feel-good endeavor that a person wants to pursue, as though obligating Christ to "strengthen" him for it. This is not what

---
88 Thayer, *Lexicon* (electronic), G842.

Paul is saying. It is Christ who commissions the work, and (then) it is Christ who strengthens the person He so commissions. It is not our place to tell God what we will do for Him ("And You will like it!"); instead, He calls each of us to whatever ministry He has planned for us (Eph. 2:10).

The Philippians' Generous Sharing (4:14–19): The Philippians "shared" in (or "communicated with") Paul's afflictions by sending him gifts of money or provisions (4:14). This was an honorable act of compassion on their part. Christians are to "Remember the prisoners [who are imprisoned for their faith], as though in prison with them, and those who are ill-treated, since you yourselves also are in the body [of Christ]" (Heb. 13:3, bracketed words are mine). In fact, this has been the Philippians' endeavor since they heard the gospel preached to them (4:15). When Paul left Philippi and traveled south to Corinth, they contributed to his financial support even to their own hurt (2 Cor. 8:1–5). Even while Paul was still in nearby Thessalonica, the Philippian church sent gifts to him (4:16). In so doing, these Christians set a high standard for all other churches—a point Paul makes to the Corinthians—regarding generosity toward Paul's ministry to the Gentiles.[89] "Not that I seek the gift itself ... " (4:17)—in other words, the money is not nearly as important to Paul as the *spiritual increase* it brings to those who supplied it *and* to the kingdom in general (2 Cor. 9:10–11, Heb. 6:10). "The gifts sent to him by the Philippians he could not refuse without insulting and offending this church. Yet he neither expected nor wanted even an occasional gift, his wealth was his contentment."[90]

While Paul did not "seek" (or personally request) the "gift" itself, he certainly did appreciate it (4:18). Because of the Philippians' generosity, "I have received everything in full and have an abundance; I am amply supplied ... ." Paul refers to these gifts as "a fragrant aroma, an acceptable sacrifice, well-pleasing to God"—i.e., not so much a gift to him as it was

---

[89] For a further exposition on this situation, I recommend my *2 Corinthians Commentary* (Spiritbuilding Publishers); go to www.spiritbuilding.com/chad.
[90] Lenski, *Interpretation*, 894.

a pleasing sacrifice to God. "The gift was a spiritual sacrifice. They were not actually buying grace, but they pleased God with this proof of their love and loyalty."[91] "Sacrifice" here alludes to the animal sacrifices that the Levitical priests offered properly and in faith (Lev. 3:5, for example). The language here also is reminiscent of what Paul has said about Christ's own sacrifice (Eph. 5:1–2)—not that the two are equal in what they accomplish, but that they are both "pleasing" to God (Heb. 13:15–16). "And my God will supply all your needs … " (4:19)—i.e., just as He has supplied Paul's needs, even though he is in difficult circumstances, God will supply the Philippians' needs, even though some of them faced "deep poverty" (cf. 2 Cor. 8:2). Since Christ has unlimited resources and offers providential help to those who believe in Him, He is more than able to take care of them.

---

91   Lipscomb, *Commentary*, 234.

Final Thoughts and Salutation
(Phil. 4:20–23)

A Brief Doxology (4:20): Overall, this has been a most positive letter. Paul has dealt little with negative matters and has had no need to correct any doctrinal errors among the Philippians themselves. His concluding remarks then, while brief, are also positive and cheerful. "Now to our God and Father … " (4:20)—in the preceding verse, Paul referred to God as "my God"; here, it is "our God." In other words, the God that Paul originally revealed to the Philippians through his gospel is the same God in whom they have come to believe. In other places, Paul refers to the gospel itself as "my gospel" (Rom. 2:16, 2 Tim. 2:8, etc.), when in fact it is "the" gospel that belongs to all those who are saved by it (Rom. 1:16). "[To Him] be the glory forever and ever. Amen"—a fitting but brief doxology (hymn of praise), as in 1 Tim. 6:15b–16. Since God is a self-existent eternal Being, He is worthy of such praise.

Greetings and a Final Exhortation (4:21–23): "Greet [lit., salute; welcome[92]] every saint in Christ Jesus" (4:21). While certain man-made religions claim the ability to *make* people "saints" (a process called beatification), the Bible teaches that *every* person who is "in Christ" is a saint to God (cf. 1 Cor. 1:2). While Paul asks the Philippians to greet Christians whom they meet, he likewise sends his greetings from those who are with him in Rome, including "those of Caesar's household" (4:22). Likely, this refers to any of the servants and guards who directly or indirectly served or protected Emperor Nero himself (ruled AD 54–68). "The term can apply to slaves and freedmen and even to the highest functionaries. Christianity has begun to undermine the throne of the Caesars."[93] It is possible that these people had learned of Paul (and subsequently heard his gospel) through connections with Philippi, a Roman colony. Or, simply by proximity to Paul's imprisonment, some had heard the gospel and then brought others to him over time (recall 1:12–13). In any case, this statement is an example of how far the gospel

---
92 Strong, *Dictionary* (electronic), G782.
93 Robertson, *Word Pictures*, 463.

had penetrated Caesar's own inner circle. It is possible—though we will never be able to confirm it—that Nero himself heard the gospel of Christ. (But if he did, it is clear through later history that he did not submit to it.)

"The grace of our Lord Jesus Christ be with your spirit" (4:23)—a common but sincere exhortation designed to draw the reader's attention back to the source of his strength and spiritual success (as in Gal. 6:18). Christ will not give His grace to those who remain outside of His fellowship but He only imparts it to those who live faithfully in covenant to God *through* Him.

Sources Used for *Philippians*

Barnes, Albert. *Barnes' Notes*, vol. 12. Grand Rapids: Baker Book House, no date.

Barnett, Paul. *Jesus & the Rise of Early Christianity*. Downers Grove, IL: InterVarsity Press, 1999.

Coffman, James Burton. *Commentary on Galatians, Ephesians, Philippians, Colossians*. Austin, TX: Firm Foundation, 1977.

Cogdill, Roy E. *The New Testament: Book by Book*. Marion, IN: Cogdill Foundation Publications, 1975.

Conybeare, W. J. and J. S. Howson. *The Life and Epistles of St. Paul*. Grand Rapids: Eerdmans, 1964.

Harrell, Pat Edwin. *The Living Word Commentary: The Letter of Paul to the Philippians*. Austin, TX: R. B. Sweet Co., Inc., 1969.

Hendriksen, William. *New Testament Commentary: Galatians, Ephesians, Philippians, Colossians and Philemon*. Grand Rapids: Baker Books, 1995.

Hester, H. I. *The Heart of the New Testament*. Liberty, MO: Quality Press, Inc., 1963.

Jamieson, Robert, Andrew Fausset and David Brown. *Jamieson, Fausset, and Brown Commentary: Commentary Critical and Explanatory on the Whole Bible (1871)*. Database © 2012 by WORDsearch Corp.

Lenski, R. C. H. *Commentary on the New Testament: The Interpretation of St. Paul's Epistles to the Galatians, to the Ephesians, and to the Philippians* (vol. 8). Peabody, MA: Hendrickson Publishers, 1998.

Lipscomb, David. *A Commentary on the New Testament Epistles, volume IV: Ephesians, Philippians and Colossians*. J. W. Shepherd, ed. Nashville: Gospel Advocate Co., 1976.

Robertson, Archibald T. *Word Pictures in the New Testament*, vol. 4. Grand Rapids: Baker Book House, no date [orig. published 1931].

Strong, James. *Strong's Talking Greek–Hebrew Dictionary*, electronic edition. Database © WORDsearch Corp.

Sychtysz, Chad. *The Holy Spirit of God: A Biblical Perspective.* Waynesville, OH: Spiritbuilding Publishers, 2010.

Thayer, Joseph. *Thayer's Greek–English Lexicon*, electronic edition). Database © 2014 by WORDsearch Corp.

Scripture taken from the NEW AMERICAN STANDARD BIBLE, Copyright 1960, 1962, 1963, 1968, 1971, 1972, 1973, 1975, 1977, 1995 by The Lockman Foundation. Used by permission.

∽ **End of *Quick Study Commentary: Philippians*** ∽

Introduction to *Colossians*

The City of Colossae: Colossae was one of three sister cities on the Lycus River in ancient Asia Minor (modern-day Western Turkey). The other two cities were Laodicea and Hierapolis (4:13); Ephesus was located about 100 miles to the west of these cities. The exact origin of Colossae is unknown, but it is recorded that at the time of Xerxes [Ahasuerus] of Persia (mid–5th century BC) it was a thriving community. The ancient Greek historian Herodotus described it (in 480 BC) as "a great city of Phrygia"; likewise, another Greek historian, Xenophon (in 401 BC), described it as "a city inhabited and prosperous and great."[94] Yet, over time, people favored Laodicea and Hierapolis over Colossae, and by the time of Paul's travels, the city was in decline.

Colossae had long been inhabited by pagan believers who worshiped various gods, as was common in the Phrygian region. Around 200 BC, Antiochus the Great brought about 2,000 Jewish families from Mesopotamia and Babylon to Lydia and Phrygia. This monotheistic influence no doubt had some positive influence on the indigenous population, but the Jews seemed more interested in the clothing industry and the "wines and baths of Phrygia" than in promoting their unique religion of Jehovah worship.[95] After 133 BC, the entire region came under control of the Roman Empire. In the 7th and 8th centuries AD, the Saracens invaded the area and devastated Colossae. The population moved to another place and deserted the city; by the 12th century AD, Colossae had disappeared.

Historical Background of *Colossians*: Likely, Paul did not establish the church in Colossae, although he might have passed through the city on his way to Ephesus prior to its establishment. Epaphras (4:12–13) is believed to be the founder of the church in Colossae and Laodicea and one of Paul's converts (see Acts 19:9–10). He may have been a native

---

94 William Hendriksen, *New Testament Commentary: Galatians, Ephesians, etc.* (Grand Rapids: Baker Books, 1995), 10–11.
95 *Ibid.*, 14.

of Colossae, and was a man of great energy, a hard–worker, and highly regarded by Paul. While Paul was under house arrest in Rome, Epaphras went to see him—a land journey of over 1,000 miles—and brought to him a report of the condition of the church in Colossae. The report was overall favorable, yet there were also reports that external teachings and philosophies threatened the spiritual stability of the group (2:8)—to be discussed below.

Authorship: Paul's authorship of this epistle has seldom been questioned. Several early church "fathers" (Justin Martyr, Theophilus, Irenaeus, Clement of Alexandria, etc.) quote liberally from this epistle, and all of them cite the apostle Paul as its author. No observant Bible student can help but notice the strong commonality between Paul's epistle to the Ephesians and the one to the Colossians. This presents a situation that is "without parallel in the New Testament. Out of 155 verses in Ephesians, 78 are found in Colossians in varying degrees of identity."[96] Both letters were written from Rome, while Paul was still in prison from his arrest in Jerusalem a few years earlier (4:3, 18). For this reason, both are considered "prison epistles" (along with *Philippians* and *Philemon*). Likely, Paul wrote both letters near the end of this imprisonment (ca. 62 AD) since Paul seems optimistic about his release. Tychicus seems to be the bearer of both letters to their intended destinations by (4:7–8).[97] Nonetheless, while *Colossians* does resemble *Ephesians* on first examination, its style and emphasis are unique. In *Ephesians*, Paul emphasizes the spiritual church of Christ; in *Colossians*, he emphasizes the Christ of the church. While these two approaches overlap, each has its own particular characteristics. Furthermore, there are several Greek phrases that appear in *Colossians* that appear nowhere else in the NT.[98]

---

[96] Charles Smith Lewis, "Ephesians, Epistle to (Relation to Other New Testament Writings)," *International Standard Bible Encyclopedia*, (© 1979 by Wm. B. Eerdmans Publishing Co.; database © 2013 by WORDsearch Corp.), electronic edition.

[97] Robert Jamieson, Andrew Fausset and David Brown, *Jamieson, Fausset, and Brown Commentary: Commentary Critical and Explanatory on the Whole Bible (1871)* (database © 2012 by WORDsearch Corp.), "Introduction to Colossians."

[98] *Ibid.*, "Introduction."

Purpose and Theme: The reason for Paul's writing this epistle appears to be self-evident. First, he wanted to give his general encouragement to these Christians. Having spent so much time in nearby Ephesus, Paul had developed several associations with believers from Colossae, some of whom are mentioned in the closing remarks and salutations. Second, Paul wished to develop in writing—as a permanent record—what has become the most detailed information on the deity of Christ (a.k.a. Christology in scholarly writings) in the NT. Robertson adds: "'The church at Colossae was the least important of any to which Paul's epistles were addressed' (Vincent). But he had no greater message for any church than he here gives concerning the Person of Christ. There is no more important message today for modern man."[99]

Certain teachers were persuading the Colossian church to believe that Christ was beneficial, but not beneficial enough, and that Christians needed to practice asceticism and other works of human effort as well to obtain righteousness before God. This idea is often referred to as the "Colossian Heresy," since it departs from the gospel that Paul taught. (A "heresy" is a human teaching, doctrine, or opinion, which departs from the divinely revealed gospel of Christ.) Lipscomb offers an excellent summary of this heresy:

> The new teachers at Colossae carefully refrained from saying anything directly opposed to the gospel. They merely called it *imperfect*, and professed to be able to supplement it. They claimed to know the way to lead the Christian beginner onward and upward to perfection; that they were able to initiate him into the mysteries of the higher life. That they could put into his hand the key of philosophy. They taught that as the flesh is the seat of sin, it must be mortified [i.e., put to death—MY WORDS]; strict dietary rules must be observed; the festivals of the Mosaic law must be observed; and in general life was to be regulated in accordance with the best human traditions. … And the gospel which Epaphras preached must be supplemented

---

[99] A. T. Robertson, *Word Pictures in the New Testament*, vol. IV (Grand Rapids: Baker Book House [no date]), 473.

> by the splendid visions of the mystic and meritorious practices of the ascetics. Redemption was not the function of Christ alone; the labor was divided among the whole host of God's angelic ministers, before whom men must bow in trembling adoration.[100]

This teaching—i.e., that the heavenly message of the gospel can successfully be married to any earthly or man–made doctrine of justification—needed to be nipped in the bud (2:8). This also explains Paul's exposition on the divine nature of Christ *and* the all–sufficiency He provides for His church. This not only benefited the Colossians but is of extreme importance to all Christians.

A third reason for writing *Colossians* remains subject to interpretation. There are many who believe that the reason for Paul's expounding upon Christ's divine nature was specifically to refute the teachings of Gnosticism—a very unchristian doctrine posing as enlightenment.

> Gnosticism, in all its forms, was characterized by belief in the evil of matter, in mediating beings, and in salvation through knowledge. Beginning with the assumption that all matter is evil, the Gnostics argued that God didn't create this world and that he has absolutely no contact with it. However, intellectual necessity did not permit them to break completely the bond between divinity and the material world. They therefore taught that God put forth from himself a series of "aeons" or emanations, each a little more distant from him and each having a little less of Deity. At the end of this chain of intermediate beings there is an emanation possessing enough of Deity to make a world but removed far enough from God that his creative activities could not compromise the perfect purity of God. … Belief in the inherent evil of matter made it impossible for the Gnostics to accept the real incarnation of God in Christ. Some of them explained it away by denying the actual humanity

---

100 David Lipscomb, *A Commentary on the New Testament Epistles: Ephesians, Philippians and Colossians*, J. W. Shepherd, ed. (Nashville: Gospel Advocate Co., 1976), 244.

of Jesus, holding that he only seemed to be human. The body of Jesus, they taught, was an illusion, a phantom, only apparently real. Other Gnostics explained away the incarnation by denying the real deity of Jesus.[101]

The problem does not lie in the historical reality of this doctrine, but in its timing and specific reference. What is formally known as "Gnosticism" did not come of age until the second century, decades after Paul's death. Yet, *early* Gnosticism was particularly Jewish in nature, since it sprang from the same non–biblical and speculative ideas that the Jews had been entertaining for years.[102] By the end of the first century, Gnosticism was making a sweep through Asia Minor and its neighboring regions. John's first general epistle (*1 John*) seems far more direct in refuting it: "Who is the liar but the one who denies that Jesus is the Christ? This is the antichrist, the one who denies the Father and the Son. Whoever denies the Son does not have the Father; the one who confesses the Son has the Father also" (1 John 2:22–23). If one has predetermined that Paul was confronting this teaching as well, then the Bible student will imagine seeing it throughout *Colossians*. However, if one reads this epistle objectively, there is nothing conclusive in linking Paul's formal defense of Christology with a rising swell of Gnostic teachers in Colossae. In fact, the epistle to the Ephesians carries a similar weight of theological apologies (i.e., formal defenses of the doctrine of God), and yet few have considered that letter to be a warning against Gnosticism. In the end, each Bible student must come to his or her own

---

[101] JFB, *Commentary* (electronic), "Introduction"; see also Robertson for excellent comments on this (*Word Pictures*, 471–2).

[102] James B. Coffman, *Commentary on Galatians, Ephesians, Philippians, Colossians* (Austin, TX: Firm Foundation, 1977), 342; Roy E. Cogdill, *The New Testament: Book by Book* (Marion, IN: Cogdill Foundation Publications, 1975), 86. "[What the Colossians faced] was not the straightforward Judaism against which the churches of Galatia had to be put on their guard at an earlier date. That Judaism was probably introduced to the Galatian churches by emissaries from Judea; this Judaism was a native Phrygian variety, which had undergone a remarkable fusion with a philosophy of non–Jewish origin—an early and simple form of gnosticism" (F. F. Bruce, "Commentary on the Epistle to the Colossians," *The New International Commentary on the New Testament: The Epistles to the Ephesians and Colossians* (Grand Rapids: Wm. B. Eerdmans Publishing Co., 1979), 166.

conclusion on the matter.

One thing is for certain: Paul expounds upon the divine nature of Christ in *Colossians* with diverse and often unique descriptions. Thus, Paul refers to Christ as the:

- Son of God's love (1:13).
- redeemer of all saints (1:15).
- visible (or incarnate) image of God (1:15).
- "firstborn" (or pre-eminence) of all Creation (1:15).
- architect of all Creation (1:17).
- head of the body (church) (1:18).
- beginning of all things (1:18).
- firstborn of the (resurrected) dead (1:18).
- embodiment of the fullness of God (1:19).
- agent of reconciliation between God and men (1:20).
- sources of all riches and wealth for men (1:27 and 2:3).
- mystery of God (2:2).
- embodiment of the fullness of the Godhead (2:9).
- head of all authorities, principalities, and powers—visible and invisible (2:10).
- One who circumcises the heart of the believer and makes him alive to God (2:11–13).
- One who removes the condemnation of law (2:14).
- substance of all the "shadows" of the Law (2:16–17).
- One who sits at the right hand of God (3:1).
- One who will be revealed with us in glory (3:4).
  substance of one's "new self" (3:10–11).
- forgiver of those who sin against Him (3:13).
- rewarder of those who serve Him (3:24).
- content (or substance) of Paul's gospel (4:3).

This is an impressive array of descriptors by any account. There can be no doubt that the central character and subject of Paul's thoughts here is none other than Jesus Christ, the Son of God. This, and subjects related to it, reverberates throughout. "In Him," "with Him," and "through Him" are common prepositional phrases that highlight Christ's direct involvement in the believer's conversion, transformation, and completion (1:28, 2:10, etc.). In any case, it is difficult to read *Colossians* without being impressed with the grandeur, loftiness, and transcendent nature of both Paul's writing and the subjects he covers. This epistle is yet another showcase of both inspired eloquence and the divinely revealed insights into the doctrine of God. Its profound character simply cannot be duplicated today without copying what Paul has already written.

General Outline

- Section One: Salutation and Paul's Praise (1:1–14)
  - Salutation (1:1–2)
  - Praise for the Colossians (1:3–8)
  - Paul's Prayer on Their Behalf (1:9–14)
- Section Two: The Divine Nature of Christ (1:15–20)
  - The Pre-eminence of Christ in the Old Creation (1:15–17)
  - The New Creation in Christ (1:18–20)
- Section Three: Standing Firm in Christ (2:6—4:1)
  - Paul's Ministry to Christ's Gospel (1:21—2:5)
  - Christ Is the Substance of One's Regeneration (2:6–15)
  - Warnings against Self–imposed Religion (2:16–23)
  - The Transcendent Christian Perspective (3:1–4)
  - Putting on the "New Self" (3:5–11)
  - Results of the Transformed Life (3:12–17)
  - Relationships in the Lord (3:18—4:1)
- Section Four: Final Remarks and Salutations (4:2–18)
  - What Is Expected of Believers (4:2–6)
  - Paul's Personal Circumstances and Salutations (4:7–18)

Section One: Salutation and Paul's Praise (1:1–12)

Salutation (Col. 1:1–2)

Paul opens this epistle characteristically by stating the ministry to which Christ had commissioned him (1:1). He is an apostle *of* Christ (one *sent* by Him) but according to the "will of God"—in agreement with the Father's divine plan. The reason for this introduction is twofold: first, it establishes the authority by which he speaks; second, it identifies him and his office to those at Colossae who may not know him. "Timothy" is Paul's beloved protégé, his "kindred spirit" (Phil. 2:20), "true child in the faith" (1 Tim. 1:2), and "beloved son" in the Lord (2 Tim. 1:2). While the letter is from both men with respect to their collaborative ministries, it clearly is written with Paul's apostolic authority. Timothy, though a co-worker with Paul, is not to be regarded as having equal authority with him.

"Saints" and "faithful brethren" (1:2) do not describe two groups of people at Colossae but are two descriptors of the same people. Those who are saints [lit., holy ones] are—in the ideal sense of the word—faithful brethren; those who are faithful brothers and sisters in Christ must necessarily be saints. "Brethren" is an old expression that comes from a Greek word [*adelphos*] which refers to those (brothers) who have come from the same womb. In a spiritual context, all who are in Christ are "brethren" (regardless of gender) since we have been born again through the same process, for the same reason, by the same divine intervention, and into the same family (John 1:12–13, 3:3–5, and 1 Peter 1:3). In a sense, the same water that served as our "grave" in which the "old man" was buried also symbolizes the watery womb of our spiritual rebirth. "Grace to you and peace"—grace and peace being divine virtues extended to those in fellowship with God.

Praise for the Colossians (1:3–8): While Paul and Timothy have never visited the church in Colossae, they nonetheless have prayed often for their welfare (1:3–4).[103] The two ministers have "heard" of their faith in God and acts of love "for all the saints" without ever having seen these demonstrated in person. Thus, as we say today, the Colossians' reputation has preceded them—in a good way. "God the Father of our Lord Jesus Christ" does not mean that God is Jesus' Father in the sense that Jesus, a Divine Being, originated from Him. As a Personage of the eternal Godhead, Jesus has *always* been in the presence of the Father (John 1:1–3). Yet in His earthly, incarnate role as the world's Redeemer, the Holy Spirit conceived Him (Luke 1:31–35) and thus He became God's "only begotten Son" (John 3:16).[104]

It is important to recognize the conditions that led to the Colossians' salvation. Their "hope" is the result of having "heard the word of truth," which is "the gospel which has come" to them through those who preach it (1:5–6; see Rom. 10:14–15 and 1 Cor. 15:1–2). They could not have had any *hope* in God apart from hearing—and, by necessary implication, *obeying*—the "word of truth" (cf. Eph. 1:13–14). "The holy gospel was at that point in time winning its supremacy over all civilized thought and it was particularly needful to warn the Colossians against the sudden growth of wild speculations, as contrasted with the unchanging, eternal truths of the gospel."[105] "Truth" here (in 1:5) cannot refer to any one particular fact or detail, but involves the entire message of God-given facts that, when received and responded to, produces salvation. Likewise, one cannot bear "fruit" *for* God unless he is in fellowship *with* God; apart from Christ no one can bear good fruit (John 15:5).

---

103 Hendriksen (*NTC*, 9), based upon the research of the eminent William Ramsay, argues that while Paul may not have been familiar with the specific members of that church, it is more than likely that Paul did pass through the city itself. The only suitable ancient land route between Antioch of Syria and Ephesus would take the traveler through Colossae, following the Meander River valley rather than a mountainous route that some commentators assume Paul took to keep him out of the city.

104 What this means is: we cannot define Jesus' pre-incarnate existence apart from His eternal existence as a Personage of the Godhead. There was never a time when Jesus did not exist as God; He was not "born" into existence as God, but only as the incarnate *Son* of God in His earthly role as our Mediator.

105 Coffman, *Commentary*, 350.

This process of salvation and its resulting "fruit" has been duplicated throughout the world in all who have heard and obeyed this same gospel. Thus, Paul says, in essence, "The reason that you have this hope is because you believed in the gospel truth; and the genuineness of your obedience is manifested in the faith and love you express in your lives." The one who originally preached this truth to the Colossians seems to have been Epaphras, whom Paul honors as "a faithful servant of Christ" (1:7–8).[106] It is through Epaphras (and others, as we will see) that Paul learned of the Colossians' faith and love. We also safely assume that it is from Epaphras that Paul has heard of the doctrinal concerns among that congregation, and the worldly philosophies that threaten to infiltrate it. "The reason that Paul puts his stamp of fullest approval on Epaphras is due to the fact that the Colossians are to remain with this teacher and are not to turn from him to the false Judaistic teachers who are trying to catch their ears and to make them learn from them."[107] The phrase "in the Spirit" (1:8) can also read "in spirit" or "in Spirit." It would seem strange that Paul would say, "Your love in {your} spirit," since this does not make sense. It is far more natural—and is consistent with Paul's typical inclusion of all three Personages of the Godhead in his references to salvation—that the Holy Spirit is meant here. Thus, these brethren have shown love to one another, but the genuine source of their love is God.

---

106 Some speculate that Paul met (and converted?) Epaphras during his lengthy stay in nearby Ephesus (JFB, *Commentary* [electronic], on 1:7). In Phile. 1:23, Paul refers to him as "my fellow prisoner," although we cannot determine conclusively whether Paul meant that literally or figuratively, or whether Epaphras was in the same prison as Paul (which seems unlikely) or was in prison elsewhere at the same time as him (which is far more plausible).

107 R. C. H. Lenski, *Commentary on the New Testament: The Interpretation of St. Paul's Epistles to the Galatians, to the Ephesians, and to the Philippians* (Peabody, MA: Hendrickson Publishers, 1998), 29; see also Hendriksen (*NTC*, 53) for similar but expounded thoughts on this.

Paul's Prayer on Their Behalf
(Col. 1:9–14)

Paul obviously has been impressed with the report he has received concerning the Colossian's faith in God and love for the brethren. "For this reason," he offers an ongoing intercessory prayer for them—a prayer that he had earlier only alluded to (in 1:3). The specific requests of his prayer include the following:

- **Knowledge of God's will (1:9).** While the Greeks prided themselves on their search for knowledge and wisdom, and Greek philosophy had been the showcase of human intellect for centuries, such knowledge was useless for improving the human condition. Sin and guilt are spiritual problems that cannot be addressed with man–made solutions, no matter how ingenious or sophisticated these appear to be. The knowledge of God's will is superior to all human knowledge because it comes from a higher source; it is not bound by human limitations; it is uncorrupted from error; it is uncompromised from self-serving interests; it leads a person to the truth which will set him free (John 8:31–32). "The maxim, 'Knowledge is power,' is true in spiritual life more than anywhere else. When a person grows in the clear knowledge of God, his strength and courage increase."[108] Knowing—and acting upon—God's eternal purpose brings a person to his full potential, inviting him into fellowship with the Godhead. "[I]n all spiritual wisdom and understanding" (1:9) far exceeds any human wisdom or earthly understanding. Divine wisdom is from above; earthly wisdom is from below; the one is infinitely superior to the other (James 3:13–17). Furthermore, "*Right* conduct cannot be the product of *wrong* knowledge."[109] While men boast in the "wisdom of the world," it is inescapably true that all such wisdom has never led anyone closer to God (1 Cor. 1:20–21). Paul's prayer, then, compels the Colossians to look upward in their thinking rather than seeking enlightenment through inferior methods of improving the human condition.

---

108 Hendriksen, *NTC*, 58.
109 Lenski, *Interpretation*, 35.

- ❑ **Walking in a manner worthy of the Lord (1:10).** Knowledge by itself is nothing until one puts it into action: the *practice* of knowledge manifests itself in visible behavior. "Walk" (in this context) refers to a lifestyle or everyday conduct that leads to a certain end—i.e., it is not aimless or directionless, but purpose-driven and goal-oriented. The word of God never instructs the Christian to choose his own "walk,"," since "a man's way is not in himself, nor is it in a man who walks to direct his steps" (Jer. 10:23). Rather, the "manner" or behavior of one's walk *in* the Lord must be consistent *with* the Lord (1 John 2:4–6). "True understanding of God's will is inseparable from living in harmony with it."[110] Whenever God has asked believers to do something in His name, He has also provided the manner in which He wants that action carried out. In other words, He does not only tell us *what* to do, He also tells us *how* to do it and gives us the *ability* to do it. Paul prays that God would not only reveal His will to the Colossians, but also that their faith would embrace this. Also, if there is a "worthy manner" in which to walk, then any "manner" that stands opposed to this is *not* worthy.
- ❑ **Pleasing God in all respects (1:10).** Striving to please God is in direct contrast with striving to please oneself (or, one's own agenda). God has declared, "To this one I will look, to him who is humble and contrite of spirit, and who trembles at My word" (Isa. 66:2b). Likewise, Jesus said, " … true worshipers will worship the Father in spirit and truth; for such people the Father seeks to be His worshipers" (John 4:23). In other words, God has revealed in His word that those who seek after Him in a worthy manner also are pleasing to Him. "[I]n all respects" means that there are no "off limits" realms in a person's heart that do not have to surrender to His will. One who knows of God *and* walks in a manner worthy of Him will relinquish control of every aspect of his life to please the One who has redeemed Him.
- ❑ **Bearing fruit in every good work (1:10).** It is never enough that a disciple of Christ merely *be* a disciple; it is necessary that his commitment to the Lord results in good "fruit." In Jesus' own

---

110 JFB, *Commentary* (electronic), on 1:10.

words, He is the Vine, we (believers) are branches, but our *objective* is not merely to serve as an ornamental fixture on the vine but to be bearers of good fruit (John 15:1–6). It is impossible to reconcile a fruitless "branch" with someone who is pleasing the Lord in all respects. The visible demonstration of discipleship is good works, not mere churchgoing or hymn-singing. It is through good works that we honor God before others (Mat. 5:16), and it is for this very purpose that we have been created anew in Christ (Eph. 2:10). We are not saved *by* works, but we cannot prove our faith in God *without* them, either (James 2:17). Thus, Paul prays that the Colossians will continue in their good works as they practice their "walk" in Christ.

- **Increasing in the knowledge of God (1:10).** Godly knowledge is not only important to have, but it needs to increase over time. The Christian must continually infuse his faith with knowledge (of God's word). Regular increase of this virtue leads to a positive and fulfilling outcome: a guaranteed entrance into the eternal kingdom (see 2 Peter 1:8–11). Failure to increase in knowledge naturally leads to spiritual atrophy and a deterioration of one's faith in God. Those who succumb to this forget about the purification of their sins (2 Peter 1:9) and become lethargic toward or distracted from their discipleship. As disciples of the Master, we are also supposed to be students of His teaching. We can accurately handle the word of God only if we know what it says and how to teach it (2 Tim. 2:15). Paul's prayer for the Colossians, then, is that they will be constantly increasing in knowledge of God rather than trying to marry human knowledge (or philosophy) with spiritual wisdom. "Everything that seems good to a man's own eyes is not good in the eyes of the Lord. Hence what God orders is the only standard of good."[111]
- **Strengthened with all power (1:11).** There is no reason to think that Paul here refers to miraculous gifts in this expression. Instead, he refers to whatever the Holy Spirit does for the human soul in preparing it to overcome worldly temptations *and* minister to God.[112] The thought here is very similar to what Paul expressed in

---

111 Lipscomb, *Commentary*, 255.

112 For a full discussion on this subject, I recommend my book, *The Holy Spirit of God: A Biblical Perspective* (Spiritbuilding Publishing, 2010); go to www.spiritbuilding.

his prayer on behalf of the Ephesians: "[I pray] that He would grant you, according to the riches of His glory, to be strengthened with power through His Spirit in the inner man … " (Eph. 3:16). It is not necessary that we know or understand *how* the Spirit strengthens the human soul; it is only important that we believe that He *does*, and that we ask God for this strengthening. A Christian is not the source of his own strength; none of us can improve or even sustain ourselves (spiritually) for walking the path of righteousness. Rather, we are instructed to "be strong *in the Lord* and in the strength of *His* might" (Eph. 6:10, emphasis added). Thus, not only are we to pray for this power, but we are to believe in what this divine power accomplishes within us.

- **Attaining steadfastness and patience (1:11).** Endurance and patience (or longsuffering) are the results of the impartation of God's strength. While God's word teaches Christians to endure in their faith (Luke 21:19, Heb. 10:36, etc.), this does not mean we possess all the energy required for this endurance. If we could empower ourselves with what is necessary to continue our walk of faith, it would not *be* faith that we would be exercising but reliance upon our own resources. "Patience" is a voluntary restraint toward something or someone in anticipation of a better outcome than one's present situation. In this way, God is patient to hold off His judgment against the world in anticipation of more people coming to repentance (2 Peter 3:9). Likewise, the believer *in* God restrains from giving in to the world, or giving up on his faith, in hope of a future reward *from* God. This is Paul's prayer for the Colossians, that they would "attain" to whatever level of endurance and patience is necessary to see their faith through to its full and rewarding conclusion (Rev. 2:10).

- **Joyously giving thanks to the Father (1:11–12).** This is as much a part of Paul's prayer for himself as it is on behalf of the Colossians. Even though living by faith in this world has its attending trials and hardships, fellowship with God is joyful and enthralling. One is external and temporary; the other is internal and everlasting (2 Cor. 4:17–18). To give thanks to God for all that He has provided the

---

com/chad.

believer, one must first recognize the joy of living in fellowship with Him (John 15:11). Likewise, one cannot truly be filled with joy who will not also give thanks for the source of his joy. Thus, "giving thanks" is not a mere obligatory or formal response to divine blessings but an outpouring of the soul's deep appreciation for the undeserved gifts it has received from a generous and benevolent God. "In Christianity, someone has said, theology is grace, and ethics is gratitude."[113]

God "has qualified" the believer for glory—he is never self-qualified or able to obtain such a future based upon his own merits (1:12). Christ's church will inherit the riches and glory that Christ Himself now enjoys. He has received all such honors as the only begotten Son, but He is willing to share these with those who have become "sons" of God by adoption (Gal. 4:4–7). (No one can receive an inheritance *from* God who is not a "son" *of* God.) One's "share [or, allotment]" reminds us of the separate tribes of Israel who all received a portion or allotment of the Promised Land (Num. 33:54). The saints' inheritance is in "in light"; in contrast, unbelievers are engulfed in a realm of spiritual darkness and ignorance (Eph. 4:17–20). "Light" is always associated with virtue or the divine nature of God, and expresses all that is excellent, pure, upright, and truthful. Not only does this speak of God's character; it defines God Himself: "This is the message we have heard from Him and announce to you, that God is Light, andx in Him there is no darkness at all" (1 John 1:5). Our inheritance, then, is not just *from* God, but is *in* God: in reality, our inheritance *is* God.

A Great Change of Allegiance (1:13–14): Just as God rescued Israel from the "iron furnace" of Egypt and brought them into the Promised Land, so He has rescued Christians from the spiritual "domain of darkness" and has brought us into the realm of light, "the kingdom of His beloved Son" (1:13). The "domain of darkness" indicates a realm in which Satan has authority over an organized and active kingdom of his own. Those who sin against God are given over to this authority, and thus to Satan's blinding and deluding influence (2 Cor. 4:3–4). This is

---

113 Bruce, "Commentary," 188.

not to say that people become prisoners of Satan in the literal sense—i.e., Satan does not own anyone's soul or have authority to send anyone to hell. However, it is accurate to say that one's sins against God warrant His condemnation, and such people become prisoners (so to speak) of Satan's *deceptions, accusations,* and *wicked influence.* We should not regard Satan as a prison warden who detains the souls of all sinners until he receives a ransom payment from God. Such depictions are unbiblical and blasphemous: God would never give His Son's blood to Satan for any reason, and we are not released from the "domain of darkness" because Satan has been paid off.[114]

This transference, then, from one domain to another refers to a change in status (or state of being) rather than a literal release from Satan's captivity. While in our condemned state of being, Satan tormented us with guilt, feelings of inadequacy, the fear of death, and the awful judgment that follows death. Christ liberates us from such torment, having removed from us the condemnation (of God) that created such incapacitating fear in the first place (Heb. 2:14–15). He has taken us *out* of one state of being (condemnation) and put us *into* another (salvation). Those condemned by God have no inheritance; they only have wages according to what they deserve—spiritual death (Rom. 6:23). Those "transferred" or translated into the kingdom of God's beloved Son receive an inheritance because they have received sonship through adoption (Acts 26:15–18). Notice the past tense of this transference: we are not *going* to be transferred, but this is a finished or completed action.[115] Barnes well summarizes this:

---

[114] For a deeper study of Satan's influence, "the darkness," and the predatory nature of this darkness, I strongly recommend my book, *This World Is Not Your Home* (Spirit-building Publishers, 2021); go to www.spiritbuilding.com/chad.

[115] Even so, this action can be reversed in the case of our faithlessness to the covenant by which we promised our loyalty to God. If we abandon our faith, then God cannot reward us with an inheritance, since He is only a rewarder of those who *are* and *remain* faithful (Heb. 11:6). Furthermore, it is not the church on earth that removes the faithless from their place in God's kingdom, but Christ alone has this authority. In other words, we can remove our personal or congregational fellowship from an impenitent Christian, but we cannot remove him (or her) from Christ's church.

> They [Christians] become subjects of a new kingdom, are under different laws, and belong to a different community. This change is made in regeneration, by which we pass from the kingdom of darkness to the kingdom of light; from the empire of sin, ignorance, and misery, to one of holiness, knowledge, and happiness. No change, therefore, in a man's life is so important as this; and no words can suitably express the gratitude which they should feel who are thus transferred from the empire of darkness to that of light.[116]

Once, we were fellow prisoners of darkness, awaiting our sentencing to our well-deserved condemnation. Now, however, "we have redemption" in Christ since His blood has provided the atonement for our sins and has released us from our condemned state of being (1:14; see Eph. 1:7 and Heb. 9:11–12). Thus, "having now been justified by His blood, we shall be saved from the wrath of God through Him" (Rom. 5:9). No one can receive forgiveness apart from a life-giving offering, because "without shedding of blood there is no forgiveness" (Heb. 9:22). No other blood has the qualities or properties that Christ's blood alone possesses; no other blood but His can impart life or redeem the human soul. Christians are redeemed because we are a blood-bought people (Rev. 5:9).

---

116 Albert Barnes, *Barnes' Notes*, vol. 12 (Grand Rapids: Baker Book House, no date), 246.

Section Two: The Divine Nature of Christ (1:15—2:5)

The Pre-eminence of Christ in the Old Creation (Col. 1:15–17)

Having spoken of the redemption that is *in* Christ, Paul now turns his attention to the pre–eminency *of* Christ (1:15–17). The power and authority that Christ possesses is exactly what we need for the task at hand. Nonetheless, no amount of human insight or exposition will be able to do justice to what Paul has to say here. "He is the image of the invisible God" (1:15)—not a reference to Christ's earthly glory, but to His glorified state following His resurrection and ascension to heaven (John 17:4–5). While the Father is invisible to us, and Christ is invisible to us now (2 Cor. 5:16), Christ remains the only historical visible expression of God (in personal form) that humankind has ever seen (2 Cor. 4:4). "He is the image" of God in His pre-incarnate state (John 1:1–2), His earthly state (John 14:7–10), and His present glorified state. It is true that Christ has never been anything *less* than this "image" in His heavenly glory regarding His divine nature (Heb. 1:3). Yet, Paul speaks of Christ's glory as it is *now* rather than His earthly ministry, and the fact that He is above all other glories or powers.

"[T]he firstborn of all creation" (1:15) *does not* and *cannot* mean that Christ was the first to *be* created. Throughout the NT, Christ is defined as one of the three Persons of the Godhead; He is a Divine Being, not a part of the Creation; He is the Creator, and the Creator cannot also be a part of the Creation; He did not create Himself.[117] Anything that is not of the Godhead has been created; the Godhead has no beginning point, but the Creation (and all *of* Creation) does; as an ever-existent Being, Christ is superior to any being that has *come into* existence at some point

---

117 The logic of this construction is inescapable. Yet, the modern Theory of Evolution claims that the material universe *did* create itself (into what it is presently), and did so apart from any outside (i.e., supernatural) intervention.

in time.[118]

Given all this, "firstborn" must mean something different here than it does in its application to ordinary human procreation.[119] Paul refers here to Christ's place before God regarding His incarnate existence. Even in His fleshly existence, He remained pre-eminent to (i.e., the premier of; in the forefront of) all that *has* been created. Thus, in this one verse (1:15), Paul expresses two sides of Christ's nature: as a Divine Being, He is the full expression of the Father; even in His human form, He remains above all other humans—and all that has been created in heaven or on earth.

"For by Him ... "—that is, by Christ the Creator (1:16). We are familiar with the *Genesis* account of Creation, in which "God" is the Creator (Gen. 1:1). Now we have an even clearer revelation: Christ *as* God is the Creator and is the reason *for* the Creation (John 1:3, 2 Cor. 8:6, and Heb. 1:3). He has created all things in the physical (or earthly) realm as well as whatever exists in the spiritual (or heavenly) realm. Christ, "existing as He did before all creation, exercises the privilege of primogeniture as Lord of all creation, the divinely appointed 'heir of all things' (Heb. 1:2). He was there when creation began, and it was for Him as well as through Him that the whole work was done."[120] While Christ's authority far surpasses all earthly authority, there are thrones,

---

[118] "There can be no doubt that the apostle here has reference to the *usual* distinctions and honours conferred upon the first-born, and means to say that, among all the creatures of God, Christ occupied a pre-eminence *similar* to that. He does not say that, *in all respects*, he resembled the first-born in a family; nor does he say that he himself was a creature, for the point of his comparison does not turn on these things, and what he proceeds to affirm respecting him is inconsistent with the idea of his being a created being himself" (Barnes, *Barnes' Notes*, 247).

[119] The Greek word used here is *prototokos*, a compound word of *proto* (foremost in time, order, or importance) and *teko* (born—literally or figuratively) (James Strong, *Strong's Talking Greek-Hebrew Dictionary*, electronic edition [database © WORDsearch Corp.], G4416; Joseph Thayer, *Thayer's Greek-English Lexicon*, electronic edition [database © 2014 by WORDsearch Corp.]; and JFB, *Commentary* [electronic], on 1:15).

[120] Bruce, "Commentary," 194. "Primogeniture" refers to an earliest ancestor, as a forefather. His role as such is symbolic, not literal, but helps to understand His primacy relative to all humankind (cf. Psalm 89:26–27).

dominions, rulers, and authorities that exist beyond our earthly view. These cannot be defined by us with any certainty: we know that they exist, but we do not know exactly what or who they are, how much power they have, or what they preside over.[121] Paul's purpose here is not to expound on the *identity* of these rulers, but only that Christ (as God) is over *all* of them.

The prepositional phrases "by Him, "through Him, and "for Him" indicate the authority, source, and purpose for all that has been created. Nothing has been created apart from Christ's direct involvement and expressed purpose. Some of us may have been conditioned to think that God the Father created humankind, and then sent His Son to redeem our fallen race.[122] However, Christ created humankind *for* His Father, and then offered *Himself* to redeem the fallen. In this way, He (Christ) could present to His Father an incomparable and priceless gift: a great assembly of blood-bought worshipers who have *chosen* to serve Him forever.

"He is before all things" (1:17)—this is Christ's pre-eminence re-stated. This also helps to define the "firstborn" reference used earlier. He is not *of* the Creation but is "before" it in every respect: in importance, authority, power, glory, and knowledge. Christ has no equal in the Creation; nothing that is created *by* the Godhead can be comparable *to* it.[123] In a real sense, Christ sits on His throne of glory at the right hand

---

121 We know Satan is well-organized and has rulers who serve under him (Eph. 6:12), but our information is scarce and shadowy. We also know that among God's angels there are different classes or levels of authority, but this information is also very limited.

122 See, for example, Isa. 66:2a, where God explicitly says that "My hand made all these things" (i.e., the heavens and earth). There is no contradiction here, however. Whatever Christ did as the Creator was certainly by the "hand" or authority of His Father, just as Moses received credit for building a tabernacle that he did not assemble, and Solomon received credit for building a temple that he did not construct. Regardless of what conclusion we reach concerning the Creation, we must never separate entirely the work of *Christ* from the work of His *Father,* as though the two Divine Persons worked independently of each other.

123 "Christ is 'firstborn' in the sense of being the unique (not created) Son of God. Christ is first *over* creation, not first *in* it. Likewise, Christ is subordinate to God the Father (1 Cor. 15:28) as his 'head' (1 Cor. 11:3) not in *nature* but in *office* or function

of His Father (Heb. 8:1–2), and all Creation bows to Him or *will* bow to Him in due time (1 Cor. 15:25–28, Phil. 2:9–11). "[A]nd in Him all things hold together"—the Greek present tense indicates that this is an ongoing, perpetual state of being.[124] Christ did not only *once* hold "all things" together (in bringing the Creation into existence) but continues to do so with His authority and power as God. *How* He holds all things together is not disclosed to us, only that He *does* this by His own sovereign will.

This much we do know: regardless of how intricately we explore the smallest atom, the most immense galaxy, or even the essence of human life, there remains a certain force that binds all things together and keeps everything in motion toward a certain end. This force is inexplicable to the scientist, physicist, astronomer, and physician; it eludes the comprehension of moralists, philosophers, and even Christians. In other words, there is a connective and cohesive element to all that has been created that holds our world together. This binding force is not something visible, quantifiable, or even comprehensible; indeed, it is something otherworldly and supernatural. This is *not* to reduce Christ's binding power to a kind of "glue" that keeps the universe intact. On the other hand, it seems clear that there is more than meets the eye, and that this invisible, binding force is nothing short of the power of the One who created all that exists.

---

as Son" (Norman L. Geisler, *Christian Apologetics* [Grand Rapids: Baker Book House, 1976], 338).
124 JFB, *Commentary* (electronic), on 1:17.

The New Creation in Christ
(Col. 1:18–20)

The Head of His Church (1:18): Not only is Christ before "all things" of the physical Creation, but He is also before all things spiritual (1:18). "While verses 15–17 unveil the Son's relationship to the old creation, this verse describes his relationship to the new creation, the church."[125] The "head" indicates the source of all intelligence, will, design, and creativity for the "body." The body does not tell the head what to do, but the head informs and directs the body. The head provides life and direction for the body and the body serves the head and carries out its will. As this is true in the natural world, so it is true in the spiritual world: Christ has supreme authority over His church; He commands, and the body responds; He defines and directs, and the church submits and obeys (Eph. 1:22–23). "Christ and His people ... are viewed together as a living unit; Christ is the head, exercising control and direction; believers are His body, individually His limbs and organs, under His control, obeying His direction, performing His work. And the life which animates the whole is Christ's risen life, which He shares with His people."[126]

Not only is He the *headship* of His church, but Christ is also its *origin* or *life-source*: His church could not have existed without Him, just as the physical Creation could not have come into existence without its Creator. "The church" does not mean "a" church (such as the church at Colossae), but "the" church—the entire body of those redeemed by the blood of the Redeemer, both living and dead. This church includes those who walked by faith before the church was built as well as those who have walked by faith ever since. This great assembly stands before God the Father and Jesus the Son amid all the angels of heaven (Heb. 12:22–24).

"He is the beginning" of His church in every respect: there is nothing in or about the establishment of His church for which Christ is not

---

125 JFB, *Commentary* (electronic), on 1:18.
126 Bruce, *Commentary*, 201.

responsible. He is the summing up of all things, including all things regarding His church (Eph. 1:9–10). "[T]he firstborn from the dead" has two concurrent meanings: Christ was the first to rise *from* the dead (without any human involvement), and He is pre-eminent over and incomparable to all those who *will be* raised from the dead. This alludes to His physical resurrection (1 Cor. 15:20–24) as well as the future resurrection of those who have died "in Christ" (1 Thess. 4:13–17). The existence of Christ's church rests upon the reality and success of Christ's resurrection from the dead. If He had not been raised, then His church will not be raised; if He could not have raised Himself (through the Father's power—see John 10:18), then He certainly could not raise us. As it is, the entirety of the church's future glory is guaranteed by the same power which Christ exercised to overcome His own death (Phil. 3:20–21). Thus, Christ has "first place in everything": He is pre-eminent over all that exists in the first Creation, as well as that of the second (or spiritual) creation. Again, there is nothing that has been created—in the physical universe, in heaven, or even in His church—over which He does not exercise supreme and absolute authority and power.

The One Who Reconciles Us with God (1:19–20): The reason for Christ's "first place in everything" is so that He can reconcile all things to the Father (1:19). In His earthly state of existence, Christ embodied the essential nature of God within Himself: God the Father was revealed, personified, and explained through the man Jesus Christ (John 1:18). The indwelling of this "fullness" was necessary because the sacrifice required for reconciliation between God and man could be satisfied only through divine effort. God's "eternal purpose" has been to provide universal salvation through His Son (Eph. 3:11–12). Through this fullness of God, Christ became not only the Creator of the old creation (i.e., the physical domain), but also of the new creation (i.e., the born-again spiritual life of believers). Thus, the "new heavens and a new earth" are realized in the spiritual context of man's fellowship with God through Christ (e.g., Isa. 65:17 and 2 Peter 3:13).

Our English word "reconciliation" is a Latin compound world that means "to be made friends with again" (1:20). The Greek word for "reconcile" means essentially the same: "to bring back to a former state of harmony."[127] We once enjoyed fellowship with God in our moral purity as children, having been born into innocence and not guilt.[128] Having "fallen" from God's holiness through having sinned (Rom. 3:23), we alienated ourselves from God and our fellowship with Him died (Eph. 2:1–3). Only through "the blood of His [Christ's] cross" are we cleansed of our sins and therefore released from divine condemnation. No longer enemies of God, we now have peace with God (or, are made sons of God by faith) (Rom. 5:8–9, Gal. 3:26–27).

Thus, Christ is the source and power of one's reconciliation to God, and every blood-bought soul has its access to (or fellowship with) God through Him. This is what Paul means whenever he speaks of being "in Christ": we enter a covenant relationship with God through Christ. In this new relationship—which we enter through being "born again" (1 Peter 1:3)—we enjoy saving grace and all spiritual blessings (Eph. 1:3). We have fellowship with the Father that is superior to what we had (in our ignorance and naivete) prior to our having sinned against Him. The relationship is restored—better than before—and will continue into eternity if we remain faithful to the covenant while we are here on earth.

Christ is the centerpiece and substance of this reconciliation; without Him, fellowship would be impossible. Peace with God comes through "the blood of His cross"—the blood which Jesus deliberately, willfully, and lovingly shed in providing Himself as a sin offering for all of humankind. His blood represents His life, since "life of the flesh is in the blood" (Lev. 17:11), and "without shedding of blood there is no

---

127 Thayer, *Lexicon* (electronic), G604.

128 Catholicism and Calvinism, for example, have long taught that people are born sinful creatures. Their position is that the entire human race has been pre-corrupted through the sin of Adam (based upon misinterpretations of Psalm 51:5, Rom. 5:12, and other passages). Given this premise, all babies are immediately sinful creatures, and must be purified either through (infant) baptism or some other means. Yet, the very concept of "reconciliation" demands that we once *were* friends of God, and that something has interrupted this friendship and must be addressed. This interruption is our personal sin against God. Notice that in every reference dealing with atonement in the gospel, we are told that we are cleansed of *our* sins, not someone else's (such as Adam's).

forgiveness of sins" (Heb. 9:22). Faith precedes forgiveness; forgiveness precedes reconciliation; reconciliation precedes fellowship with God; and fellowship precedes salvation. In other words, these factors are not only part of our salvation, but they must also be conducted or implemented in the right sequence. No one could expect to be reconciled, for example, who was not first forgiven of his sins, and no one could be forgiven unless Christ had first provided His blood as an agent of atonement.

To clarify: *we* are reconciled to *God*—He is not reconciled to us. God has not moved, changed, or declined in any way, but *we* have through the act of our sin. Yet, this reconciliation is what God has always wanted (Isa. 53:10–12) and is what human beings have always needed (Rom. 5:10–11, 2 Cor. 5:18–19).[129] "[W]hether things on earth or ... heaven" (1:20)—i.e., whatever sin had unbalanced in the lives of men on earth or the souls of men in heaven is corrected through Christ's redemptive work. This redemption of sinful people also corresponds to the redemption of all Creation (Rom. 8:19–23): as individual believers are redeemed, so the entire Creation—i.e., the *purpose* for which the Creation came to be—is fulfilled.

---

129 For an exposition on the "ministry of reconciliation," I recommend my 2 Corinthians Commentary (Spiritbuilding Publishers, 2010) on the passage cited; go to www.spiritbuilding.com/chad.

Section Three: Standing Firm in Christ (1:21—4:1)

Paul's Ministry to Christ's Gospel (Col. 1:21—2:5)

Having clarified what God has done to secure our reconciliation to Him, Paul now turns to the believer's personal responsibility in the matter. First, our separation from God due to sin is *real* and *humanly insurmountable* (1:21). Paul uses three terms or phrases to depict this.

- ❑ **"alienated"**: This means to be estranged to or a non–participant (with someone).[130] Sin is the cause for separation between man and God; yet separation could not have occurred unless a relationship had once existed. In other words, we cannot separate *from* God unless we had once enjoyed *unity* with Him (and we cannot be reconciled to Him unless a separation had first occurred). This union cannot allude to that which Adam himself once enjoyed with God while in the pristine Garden of Eden. The sin that created the breach is *personal*—i.e., Paul tells the Colossians that it was *their* sins that separated them from God, not Adam's or anyone else's (cf. Eph. 2:1). No one's fellowship with God can be corrupted because of another person's sin (cf. Deut. 24:16 and Ezek. 18:23, in principle). Modern concepts of "original sin" or "total hereditary depravity" stand opposed to these simple yet profound premises.[131]

- ❑ **"hostile in mind"**: This hostility (or enmity) comes from a decision to seek friendship with the world at the expense of one's relationship with God (Rom. 8:6–8, James 4:4). In other words, the sinner does not exist in a neutral or compatible state of existence with God but

---

130 Strong, *Dictionary* (electronic), G526.

131 For a fuller discussion on Calvinism (or, The Doctrine of Predestination), I recommend reading Chapter 17 in my book, *The Gospel of Saving Grace* (Spiritbuilding Publishers, 2020); go to www.spiritbuilding.com/chad.

has become His opponent and is antagonistic to His will: "He who is not with Me [Jesus] is against Me; and he who does not gather with Me scatters" (Mat. 12:30). "In mind" does not soften the effect of this hostility toward God: the damage is not merely a conceptual one but is real and—if not properly addressed—eternally ruinous. We might think of the condition of those in the antediluvian world whose "every intent of the thoughts of [their hearts] was only evil continually" (Gen. 6:5, bracketed words added). While the sinner's heart may not be *continually* dwelling on wickedness, nonetheless he remains a wicked person no matter how much good he may perform on his own. No one can overcome his own spiritual dilemma through human effort. If we could, then we would not need the grace of God to save us—we could simply save ourselves.

❏ **"{engaged} in evil deeds"**: The Greek sentence here reads something like, "You were enemies of God as manifested through your wicked works."[132] The practice of evil deeds—however small or insignificant they might seem to the one responsible for them—only underscores the reality of the problem. Just as good fruit cannot come from a bad tree (cf. Mat. 7:16–20 and 12:33–35), so "fruit of the Spirit" (Gal. 5:22–23) cannot come from an enemy of God.[133]

Reconciliation Remains Conditional (1:22–23a): "Yet now" indicates a radical change in this former state of being (1:22). The *point of reference* for our reconciliation with God is the real, historical, and atoning sacrifice that Christ made upon His cross. If He had not literally died on that cross, no change in our state of being would be possible; we would still be enemies of God.[134] Christ did not just offer blood

---

132 Marvin Vincent says that the "performance" of a wicked mind is outwardly exhibited in one's wicked works (*Word Studies*, electronic edition [database © 2014 by WORDsearch Corp.], on 1:21).

133 It is true that even wicked people can perform incidental good deeds that appear to conform to the "fruit of the Spirit," but it is impossible for such people to achieve friendship with God through such works. A few good deeds do not make one a Christian, cannot cleanse the human conscience of its guilt, and cannot remove the divine condemnation upon one's soul. Only the blood of Christ can do these things (Heb. 9:11–14), and no one can receive the blood of Christ without obedience to the word of God *and* submission to the Spirit of God.

134 The same can be said of Christ's resurrection: " … if Christ has not been raised,

(recall 1:20), but also His entire body; thus, the sinner is reconciled not through the body *or* the blood, but through both the body *and* the blood of Christ (Heb. 10:5–10). We cannot separate the importance of His blood (as an agent of atonement) from the importance of His body (as an agent of the sacrifice itself). Thus, the two thoughts run concurrently in Scripture: "In Him we have redemption through His blood, the forgiveness of our trespasses, according to the riches of His grace" (Eph. 1:7) and "By this will [of God] we have been sanctified through the offering of the body of Jesus Christ once for all" (Heb. 10:10, bracketed words added). Now that we have been sanctified through the bodily offering of God's Son, the "fruit" we bear for Him is no longer "fruit for death," but is "fruit for God" (Rom. 7:4–5).

"[I]n order to present you … " (1:22) indicates the *purpose* for this reconciliation. We cannot make ourselves holy, blameless, or beyond reproach; these are things that must be done for us. God is the One who credits a person with righteousness based upon that person's obedient faith in Him (as in Rom. 4:3 and Gal. 3:6). Christ's reconciliation of the sinner's soul puts him in favorable standing with God; instead of guilt, the sinner–turned–saint now enjoys innocence that he does not deserve yet desperately needs.

The small word "if" (1:23a) has tremendous bearing upon the long-term success of the one who comes to God for salvation. "If" means this relationship with God is conditional: *if* one remains faithful, it continues perpetually; *if* he does not, however, then he forfeits all that God has promised him. Such language defeats the fictional belief of being "once saved, always saved" or an infallible "preservation of the saints"—teachings of Calvinism, not Scripture. If salvation is dependent upon *any* human effort, then it is conditional and not irrevocable.

To clarify: God's *promises* are guaranteed and cannot change; yet the believer's faith is the variable that can change the imparting of those

your faith is worthless; you are still in your sins" (1 Cor. 15:17). Thus, it is not enough that Christ died, if indeed He has not been resurrected; on the other hand, He could not have been literally resurrected unless He had in fact died. The two actions either stand or fall together, and we cannot preach the one without the other (1 Cor. 15:3–4).

promises. The expression "in the faith" here (1:23a) does not merely mean "faithful" (without a specific point of reference) but faithful *to* something mutually valued by both parties (i.e., the Christian and God).[135] In this case, "the faith" refers specifically to the gospel which has been preached throughout the Roman Empire—"in all creation under heaven" being a broad phrase that simply means "everywhere."[136] The believer is not to remain true to this gospel message in a superficial or casual sense, but he is to be "firmly established and steadfast" (or, grounded and settled)—i.e., constantly increasing in knowledge, maturity, and demonstrations of faithfulness (see comments on 2:6–7).

Paul's Ministry and Proclamation (1:23b–29): At this point (1:23b), Paul shifts his discussion from the details of the gospel itself to familiarize the Colossians with his part in the preaching of that gospel. "I, Paul, was made a minister"—not, "I appointed myself" or "the church ordained me," but (by implication), "Someone with authority greater than men commissioned me to be a spokesman for this message." Indeed, Christ directly commissioned Paul for this purpose (Acts 9:15–16), a point which Paul has made in the openings to his other epistles (Rom. 1:1, 1 Cor. 1:1, etc.). The purpose of this information is not to boast or assert any personal merit, but to provide *authority* and thus *credibility* to that which he writes. Since he has never met many of the Christians at Colossae, it is necessary that they know who he is and what business he must write to them concerning doctrinal matters and other instructions. "Minister" comes from the Greek *diakonos*, the same word translated elsewhere as "servant" (Rom. 16:1) or "deacon" (1 Tim. 3:8). In a sense, Paul is a specialized deacon in the church, and all ministers of the gospel today are to imitate his servitude (though they have not been given his authority).

---

135 Some manuscripts read "in faith," which would mean "according to a person's faith in God." This does not change the outcome. To be "in *the* faith" one must be faithful to what "*the* faith"—the gospel—teaches. No one can be considered "faithful" to God who does not conform to His Son's gospel (1 John 2:3–6).

136 "Pliny, not many years subsequent to the writing of this epistle, wrote to the Emperor Trajan (B. X. Ep. 97) saying, 'Many of every age, rank, and sex are being brought to trial. For the contagion of that superstition [i.e., Christianity] has spread over not only cities, but villages and the country'" (JFB, *Commentary* [electronic], on 1:23; bracketed word is mine).

No doubt, too, the news of Paul's troubles and persecutions (as a direct result of his commission to be a minister of the gospel) has already reached the ears of the church in Colossae (1:24). A natural question might be, "If Paul's message is from God, then why is he facing such resistance?" Historically, the prophets of God have always faced resistance from those who oppose His will, but this fact may not be understood by Gentile believers (unfamiliar with the OT) as well as it is with Jewish believers. Thus, the need for clarification and explanation is in order. Paul responds, in essence, "I do suffer for what I preach, but my suffering *benefits* you—it does not in any way detract from the *genuineness* of the message" (paraphrase of 1:24a). While Christ was crucified in the flesh, Paul also suffers in the body—not equally to Christ's suffering, but as a complement or an accompaniment to it (cf. Phil. 3:10).[137] Christ suffered in the flesh to establish and build His spiritual church; Paul suffers to propagate the work of that church and preach its gospel. Put another way: Christ suffered *in* His body for the salvation of believers everywhere; Paul suffers *for* His body (Christ's church) to propagate this salvation through his ministerial work. "[F]illing up what is lacking in Christ's afflictions" (1:24b) cannot mean that Christ did not suffer enough (and Paul must complete what He did not finish); such logic contradicts the once–for–all redemptive work of Christ (Heb. 10:10, 1 Peter 3:18, etc.). What it means in this context is that Paul viewed his suffering (and that of all genuine ministers) as being supportive of and necessary for the overall preaching of Christ's gospel (cf. 2 Tim. 2:8–10 and 3:12).

Thus, Paul was made a minister of Christ's church (as a "stewardship" bestowed upon him—see 1 Cor. 4:1–2) to provide to others what Christ had revealed to him (1:25–27). This revelation was once a "mystery"—a message that remained hidden until the time it was to be unveiled—but now it has been made known (or manifested) to believers everywhere.

---

[137] "When Paul is so concerned as he is here to assert the sole sufficiency of Christ as Saviour [*sic*] and Mediator, it would be absurd to suppose that the means that he himself, by the hardships he endures, is in some way supplementing the saving work of Christ. Paul is as sure as the writer to the Hebrews [Heb. 10:10] was that Christ's saving work was accomplished 'once for all' by His obedience unto death" (Bruce, *Commentary*, 216; bracketed words are mine).

The mystery does not only involve the terms and conditions of the gospel itself, but specifically the universal salvation offered to "the Gentiles" as well as the Jews (see Eph. 3:1–12). "Mystery" is thus set opposed to revelation: the word of God was once obscure, but now it has been revealed "to His saints." Moses and the prophets revealed only shadows, types, and glimpses of what was to come; Christ and His apostles have declared the substance of God's salvation to humankind. "Gentiles" refers to all people who are not Jews: prior to the revelation of Christ's gospel, fellowship with God was proclaimed only through the Jews and their Law. Now, however, God invites *all* people into His fellowship through the same message, same method, and same Savior (Rom. 1:16).

"[W]hich is Christ in you" (1:27) indicates the indwelling of Christ, which is not a separate indwelling than that of the Spirit but speaks of the same action: the divine presence of God in the heart and life of the believer (Rom. 8:9). No one can have Christ "in" him without also having God's Spirit: if one Personage of the Godhead abides in Him, so must the others.[138] Christ is "in" those who believe in, love, and obey Him: "it is no longer I who live, but Christ lives in me" (Gal. 2:20). Thus, Christ abides in those who give allegiance to Him, and they also abide in Him (John 15:7–10, 1 John 3:24, 4:16, etc.).

"[W]e proclaim Him"—"proclaim" is from the same Greek root word from which we get "evangelism"; "we" refers to Paul and all other evangelists who announce the revealed word of God to men. This word serves several purposes (as in 2 Tim. 3:16–17):

- ❑ As an admonition (or warning) for those whose souls stand in jeopardy with God. The warning here is to repent of sin while there is still opportunity, and not to allow the heart to grow hardened by the deception of sin (Heb. 3:12–15).

---

138 For a fuller study on the Holy Spirit, I strongly recommend my book, *The Holy Spirit of God: A Biblical Perspective* (Spiritbuilding Publishers, 2010); go to www.spirit-building.com/chad.

- ❑ As the source of sound teaching (or doctrine) according to the revealed wisdom of God, even though this appears inferior to those who resist it (1 Cor. 1:18–21).
- ❑ As the preparation for one's presentation before God. Christ does His part in atoning for and sanctifying the human soul (recall 1:22), but each believer is to do *his* or *her* part as well. We are never asked to do what Christ alone can perform; yet Christ does not do for us what we are to perform in faith.

The threefold "every man" phrases (1:28) are not mere redundancies but underscore the critical need for the preaching and teaching of the word of God. No person ("man") is "complete in Christ" apart from *learning* and *implementing* the revealed instruction that comes from heaven—no exceptions. (Whether Paul intended it, this refutes the view that "completion" in Christ is exclusive with those who possess allegedly mystical knowledge, as Gnostics maintained.) "Complete" means mature, full-grown, or perfect (depending upon the context). The source of this completion lies outside of the believer's own ability to achieve it. "In Christ" is one of Paul's favorite expressions throughout his epistles. It refers to living in union or fellowship with God the Father through Christ the Son. This is accomplished when both parties (God and the believer) enter a covenant agreement, the terms of which are spelled out in the gospel.

Paul labors to bring about God's word to whomever will hear it, but he does not work according to his own power. Instead, he strives to fulfill his ministry "according to His power, which mightily [or, powerfully] works within me" (1:29). Paul may refer here to the *miraculous* power that works within him, yet when we compare this with similar passages (Eph. 3:20, Phil. 1:6, 2:13, etc.), this can easily mean the everyday work of divine grace in the heart of the believer. Paul's "striving"[139] is not against *God's* will but is against all those forces or people that would oppose it (2 Cor. 10:5). We are never told to strive against God, but we most certainly must strive to conform to Him.

---

139 "Striving" is from the Greek word *agonizomai*, from which we get our English word "agonize"; see Luke 13:24 and 1 Cor. 9:25, where the same Greek word is used.

Paul's Concern for Those Whom He Does Not Know (2:1–5): Many of the Christians at Colossae had not met Paul, yet he has exerted a great deal of effort on their behalf (2:1). He tells them this not to boast or gain sympathy, but so that they can support him (through prayer, encouragement, and whatever other means) and so that they will respect his authority. These words are not exclusive to those at Colossae, but also to the saints in nearby Laodicea (see comments on 4:16) and all other Christians who have not met him personally, such as those in Hierapolis (see 4:13). In other words, "Even though we have not met, I want you to know that I, as an apostle of God, am interested in you and seek your best interest through prayer and the preaching of Christ's gospel."

This preaching has not been a passive interest, but a "great struggle" (or, strenuous conflict), some of which is detailed in 2 Cor. 11:25–29. Paul's purpose is not to divide, which is the agenda of false teachers (in separating believers from the word and dividing believers from each other). Rather, it is to unify (or "knit together") all believers in "the wealth that comes from the full assurance of understanding" the word of God (2:2). In other words, the purpose of an evangelist is not to keep Christians in the dark and teach only limited information, but to declare the "whole purpose of God" (Acts 20:26) and to immerse them in what Christ has revealed from heaven. Put another way: an evangelist is not to exercise authority over Christians through the control (or manipulation) of information but is to provide them with everything they need to know. Encouragement and understanding, not sophistry or power struggles, are proper objectives. This results in increasing understanding of Christ Himself, in whom are priceless treasures of *knowledge* (as facts and information) and *wisdom* (as the proper application of that knowledge) (2:3). These treasures, though "hidden" in Christ, are meant to be discovered by those who draw near to Him in faith.

Paul clearly states his purpose for writing to the Colossians (2:4–5): he does not want them to be seduced by (or, overtaken with) any "persuasive argument" that would oppose the gospel that he preaches. These foreign persuasions, which no doubt posed as having apostolic authority, had infiltrated Colossae, Laodicea, Hierapolis, and other cities of Phrygia and Asia Minor. "Paul is here referring to the false teachers, who attempted to mix Oriental theosophy, angel worship, and Jewish asceticism with pure Christianity."[140] "Stability of your faith" indicates a faith that is not wavering, failing, or filled with contradictory teachings. This thought leads into the next section, which deals with *how* one's faith is stabilized and made steadfast.

---

140 JFB, *Commentary* (electronic), on 2:4. "Theosophy" refers to the (alleged) doctrine of God that is based upon mystical insight or specially revealed revelation.

Christ Is the Substance of One's Regeneration (Col. 2:6–15)

Walking and Growing in Christ (2:6–7): "Therefore … " (2:6) indicates a new thought built upon the previously laid foundation. The Colossian Christians had not merely received the gospel of Christ (as a message), but they had received Christ Himself (as an indwelling). Paul refers to the Colossian Christians' reception of Christ in the past tense: now that it has happened, a certain kind of thinking and lifestyle is to follow ("so walk in Him"). There must be union or harmony between one's inward profession of faith and his outward conduct. "[H]aving been firmly rooted" (2:7) seems to jar against the "so walk in Him" concept, as if Paul has just unwittingly mixed his metaphors. How can a person "walk" and be "firmly rooted" all at once? This question is resolved when we understand that Paul is talking about two different things. What is "firmly rooted" (in this context) is the believer's *faith*—i.e., it is not going anywhere—while the "walk" refers to his *conduct*. This person's faith has taken root downward in Christ for stability, and thus is able to grow upward toward heaven. (We are not to take the "downward" and "upward" directions literally, of course.) A tree that is firmly rooted, for example, is thus able to grow in height and girth with no fear of toppling over (Psalm 1:3).

Thus, Paul commends the Colossians for having rooted themselves in Christ, but now he encourages them to follow through with the natural growth process. The "walk" will be the outward and visible demonstration of that inward faith. One's faith is like a living, breathing, growing organism; one's Christian life is like a healthy, rhythmic cadence of activity that leads toward a certain goal—a journey that winds through this life and into the life to come. "[J]ust as you were instructed" indicates the uniformity and consistency of the doctrinal basis for this indwelling and walking. The Colossians did not hear a different gospel than did all other believers but the same message that led to the same inescapable conclusions (recall 1:5). This walk is to be "overflowing with gratitude," indicating the necessary attitude the believer must have to appreciate and embrace all that God has done for him. No one can enjoy Christ's indwelling by his own volition; no one can walk the pathway to heaven by his own strength. Gratitude certainly involves the giving of thanks but also necessarily implies reverence and respect. When it comes to the believer's disposition toward God, gratitude and reverence go together. The opposite is also true: ingratitude and irreverence also go together.

Avoiding Worldly Philosophies (2:8): While the Colossians are established in Christ (as though rooted in sacred ground), the possibility remains that they could be taken prisoner to somewhere else (as though uprooted and taken captive to a foreign land). This seems the clearest and most natural flow of thought from the preceding verses to the present one (2:8). If the believer does not remain completely grounded in Christ, then he will become the prisoner (or spoil) of someone else's inferior teaching. Paul mentions several dangers of which the Christian must beware:

- **philosophy** [lit., love of wisdom]. Likely, this refers to Jewish philosophy (or sophistry), which involves extra-biblical teachings, mystical superstitions, strict asceticism, rituals of purification, and other man-made teachings intended to impart greater wisdom upon the one who accepts them. Whether Paul specifically refers to Gnostic teachings cannot be known for certain, but "philosophy" certainly could apply to this (see "Introduction"). In any case, human philosophy has long paraded itself as the key to higher wisdom and (often) moral superiority, even though it rests upon the finite perspectives and flawed thinking of men.
- **empty deception.** This broad category covers any human teaching that claims to impart enlightenment, wisdom, secret knowledge, etc., yet is devoid of anything useful or practical. Such teachings claim to bring one closer to God (or one's version of "God") yet stand opposed to what He has in fact revealed.
- **tradition of men.** "Tradition" here [Greek, *paradosis*] means any teaching transmitted from one person to another, whether by word

of mouth or writing.[141] Likely, Paul refers either to Jewish traditions (wrongly made tantamount with the teachings of God; see Mat. 15:1–9) or those of Greek philosophers, rhetoricians, and other promoters of human wisdom.[142]

- **elementary principles of the world.** "Elementary" refers to the first things (in a series) from which all other things (in that series) are derived. Our modern vernacular would read, "The ABCs of language," or "The simplest and primary physical components of the universe."[143] In a sense, Paul refers to the simple, child–like, and rudimentary building blocks of human knowledge (as in Gal. 4:3). While philosophers are prone to tout their teachings as being wise and profound, Paul discredits these as being nothing more than infantile understandings in comparison to what the believer discovers in Christ.

Christ and His revealed wisdom is the ultimate standard against which all man–made teachings are to be compared (1 Cor. 1:30). The "rather than" phrase indicates making a deliberate choice between Christ and human wisdom. Comparatively, it matters little what men produce on their own; no amount of human logic or wisdom can erase a single human sin or redeem a single human soul. What God has revealed from heaven is more excellent and of far greater value than anything that is of this world (cf. James 3:13–18). "Christ is the measure for all human knowledge since he is the Creator and the Sustainer of the universe."[144]

Spiritual Completion Is "in Him" (2:9–10): The *reason* why Christ and His gospel are superior to this world is because He Himself was not

---

141 Thayer, *Lexicon* (electronic), G3862.

142 "The false teachers boasted of a higher wisdom in theory, transmitted by tradition among the initiated; in practice they enjoined asceticism, as though matter and the body were the sources of evil. Phrygia (in which was Colosse) had a propensity for the mystical and magical, which appeared in their worship of Cybele and subsequent Montanism [Neander]" (JFB, *Commentary* [electronic], on 2:8).

143 This is the actual reference Peter uses for this same word in 2 Peter 3:10, 12. In that passage, Peter refers to the reduction of the earth (i.e., the entire physical system) to its initial, primary, most basic elements through the application of intense heat.

144 Robertson, *Word Pictures*, 491.

entirely *of* this world (2:9). "In Him" in this specific context means "in the physical person of Christ on earth," His bodily manifestation before men (John 1:14–18, 1 John 1:1–3). The "fullness of Deity"[145] refers to "the totality of God's nature and person."[146] Jesus was not half–God and half–man; rather, He was a very real Personage of God dwelling in a very real person of this world. He was the Son of God, and at the exact same time He was the Son of Man—the fullness of the Godhead as well as the fullness of (what it means to be) a human being. Such information is not meant to be humanly comprehensible, but Paul provides this to prove that it is far *superior* to whatever people produce otherwise. The fact that it *is* incomprehensible illustrates Paul's very point: the inferior, elementary, and hopeless teachings of men cannot hold a candle to the full essence of God in human form.[147]

"[A]nd in Him [i.e., Christ] you have been made complete" (2:10a)—which means, *apart* from being "in Him," a person remains incomplete and thus unprepared for his presentation before the Father (recall 1:22). The "in Him" phrase *here* now is meant spiritually, since Paul is no longer dealing with Jesus' physical body but His spiritual body (the

---

145 Literally, "the Godhead," from *theotes* (Strong, *Dictionary* [electronic], G2320), used only here in the NT. Deity is separated from the Creation: whatever is not Deity (the Father, Son, and Holy Spirit) is a creation *of* Deity, and whatever is Deity cannot be created but has a self-generated, ever-present, and eternal existence. Paul's point speaks to the great paradox of Christ's incarnation: the time when Deity became one with the Creation through the human person of Jesus Christ. "The fullness of the Godhead [dwelt] in Him *in a bodily way, clothed the body*. This means that it [dwelt] in Him as one having a human body. This could not be true of His preincarnate state, when He was 'in the form of God,' for the human body was *taken on* by Him in the fullness of time, when 'He *became* in the likeness of men' (Phil. 2:7), when the Word *became* flesh. The fullness of the Godhead dwelt in His person from His birth to His ascension" (Vincent, *Word Studies* [electronic], on 2:9; bracketed words are mine).

146 JFB, *Commentary* (electronic), on 2:9.

147 Let us not make the mistake of agnostics (for example) and assume that "incomprehensible" necessarily means "impossible." Quantum physics may seem incomprehensible to you, but it is a fact of the physical universe. On the other hand, a four–sided triangle is not only incomprehensible but is impossible; or a Minotaur is comprehensible (in the human imagination) but is impossible (to exist). The point is: we need to maintain the right *context* when expounding upon what is (or seems) humanly incomprehensible.

church—recall 1:18). Thus, we see both sides of the picture: "in Him," the believer receives what is necessary for his salvation; at the same time, he is in the constant state of *achieving* completion through the constant nourishment of his faith (recall 1:28). The one (salvation) is dependent upon the other (genuine faith), yet both are made possible only through Christ's direct intercession.

"[A]nd He is the head of all rule and authority" (2:10b)—a reiteration of what Paul said earlier (in 1:16–17; cf. Eph. 1:22–23). If Christ possesses the power to bring the Creation into existence and rule over it with absolute authority, He certainly has the power and authority to redeem the human soul that trusts in Him for salvation. Likewise, if Christ is above any created being (whether angels or men), it is foolish to worship the creation above or instead of the Creator (Rom. 1:22–25). If Christ is sufficient for one's salvation, it is unnecessary to look outside of Christ for something else for one's completion.[148] As pointed out earlier, Paul emphasizes one's spiritual union with Christ: "in Him," "with Him," and "through Him." Christ is not merely a participant in the process of one's salvation; He is the reason for and substance of it.

Spiritual Circumcision of the Heart (2:11–12): Having defined the way things are *presently* for the Colossians, Paul then reminds them of the way things *were* (2:11). It is true that the Colossian church was comprised mainly of uncircumcised Gentile believers, yet the "circumcision" he mentions here is spiritual in nature, not literal. The Judaists—those who tried to impose ordinances of the Law of Moses upon Gentile converts—insisted that all believing males be circumcised. Yet, this was not required by the gospel of Christ and did nothing for one's justification.[149] In Christ, *every* believer is "circumcised"—men and

---

148 This is the claim of Gnostics and other parasitical religionists that use the Christian gospel as a vehicle to promote their own teachings. Gnosticism (for example) necessarily implies that to be a Christian is noble but remains inferior to the fuller knowledge or higher understanding that comes through secret information and mystical insight. If Paul *is* refuting Gnosticism in this letter, then he is doing so most directly at this point (2:10).

149 See Acts 15:1–11 for the historical perspective of this subject. I also recommend my *Galatians and Ephesians Commentary* (Spiritbuilding Publishing, 2012) for a de-

women, Jew and Gentile, master and slave—but not with human hands, and not in the flesh. Instead, all are "circumcised" by the (symbolic) cutting away of the "old self" in order that a new life can begin.[150] This is an action only Christ can do, since it requires supernatural power and authority to perform it. No person can remove the corrupted "old self" of another, nor can he remove his own corrupted self. This must be carried out by One whose authority and ability far exceeds any human effort.

When did this "circumcision" occur? Paul explains it precisely: upon one's water baptism into Christ (2:12). In other words, Christ does in baptism what only He (as God) is able to do, yet He is not baptized for us and He will not "circumcise" us if we are not baptized. It is incorrect to say that "baptism replaces circumcision," for this confuses what Christ does with what the believer does. Believers must be baptized in water to be "in Christ"; Christ circumcises the heart *of* each believer in this physical demonstration of his faith in Him.[151] Christ's "removal" of the "body of the flesh" is not accomplished by mere immersion in water; likewise, immersion in water means nothing without one's spiritual circumcision by Christ. Nonetheless, the two actions—what Christ does for the believer and what the believer does for Christ—happen simultaneously. Thus, the one being baptized believes that Christ does for him what he could not do for himself: salvation is by divine grace,

tailed explanation of this; go to www.spiritbuilding.com/chad.

150 According to the Law of Moses, a male child was circumcised on the eighth day of his life (Lev. 12:3). For the first seven days, he belonged solely to his mother and father; after this, however, he was made a citizen of the nation of Israel and a recipient of God's promises to that nation. In other words, circumcision—with its cutting of the flesh (i.e., removal of the foreskin of the penis), shedding of blood, and permanent (and irreversible) change—represented that child's new beginning with God. This new beginning is also indicated by the "eighth day" in which it occurs: the number eight in Scripture often is used to symbolize a new life, new power, new dynasty, or new beginning. For all these reasons, circumcision becomes an ideal illustration by which to define the new life of the believer "in Christ."

151 This is parallel to what Jesus said to Nicodemus in John 3:3–5: the believer is "born again" through an act of faith (his baptism—the "water" in that passage) *and* an act of God (summed up as "the Spirit"), not one or the other. No one is "born again" only through baptism, nor is one "born again" only through God acting on his heart apart from his God-ordained demonstration of faith.

but through his faith. The outward or visible sign of the believer's faith is his baptism.[152]

One who *is* baptized no longer belongs to himself but to God. His baptism is the visible demonstration of his having entered into a covenant agreement with Him. This covenant comes to life by the blood of Christ (Mat. 26:27–28, Heb. 9:15–25) and becomes binding upon the believer in his baptism. (We can baptize people, but we cannot *un*–baptize them: the decision, once made, is for life.) Through baptism, the believer calls upon the name of the Lord to save him (Acts 2:21, 4:12, 22:16, etc.); in the process of baptism, Christ performs His supernatural work upon that person's heart. Thus, we see both aspects of one's salvation: that which the believer performs, and that which God alone can perform (cf. John 3:3–5 and Heb. 10:19–22). By participating in a symbolic death, burial, and resurrection process of our conversion, we are united with Christ in the likeness of His own death, burial, and resurrection (Rom. 6:3–7, 2 Tim. 2:11). Our baptism is literal, even though our "death" is symbolic (or, spiritual in nature); Christ's death was literal, even though His characterization of it as a "baptism" was figurative (Mark 10:38). As necessary as it was that Christ died and was resurrected, so it is necessary that the believer share in that process to identify with Him.

The Believer's 'Debt' Is Canceled (2:13–15): "[W]hen you were dead" (2:13) indicates the believer's pre-converted state of being (cf. Eph. 2:1–3). Even though human perception does not fully comprehend this deadness, it is real, nonetheless. Paul speaks here of the soul's condemnation before God: he is as a dead man—he is like a "dead man walking," like a condemned convict on his way to the execution chamber. This "dead" person has no future life with Him; he is dead to *God* even while he lives in this *world* (Eph. 4:17–19 and 1 Tim. 5:6, in principle). (Paul specifically refers to Gentiles here, since they are

---

152 There are *other* signs as well, such as obedience, repentance, confession, etc., but Paul only focuses on baptism here. In Rom. 10:9–10, for example, he only focuses on belief and confession, but this does not nullify the need for other demonstrations of faith prescribed elsewhere. There is *no single passage* in the NT that details for the believer *all* that he must do to be "in Christ." "The sum of Your word is truth" (Psalm 119:160), not the dissected parts of it.

regarded as the "uncircumcised"; however, the application in principle extends also to Jews who face the same condemnation.) The only way to escape this condemned state of being is to put that condemned "man" (the "old self") to death and begin a new life "in Christ."

> But baptism not only proclaims that the old order is over and done with; it proclaims that a new order has been inaugurated. The convert did not remain in the baptismal water; he emerged from it to begin a new life [see Rom. 6:3–4]. Baptism, therefore, implies a sharing in Christ's resurrection as well as in His death and burial.[153]

Being "made alive" in Christ necessarily involves the forgiveness of one's sins (Eph. 1:7, 2:4–5), since one state of being cannot occur apart from the other. "To cure our death, God made us alive; to deliver us from sins, he quickened us [lit., made us alive] together with Christ."[154]

God's condemnation of the sinful soul is the "certificate of debt" that was "hostile" to that person's spiritual well-being (2:14). This certificate (or handwriting) refers to all the decrees or details of transgressions which the sinner has incurred. Jesus nailed this decree of condemnation to His cross: in effect, He absorbed in Himself, by means of His own sacrificial death, the penalty incurred by the sinner.[155] "Canceled" here

---

153 Bruce, *Commentary*, 235–236; bracketed words are mine.

154 JFB, *Commentary* (electronic), on 2:12; bracketed words are mine.

155 Many have assumed that this "certificate" was the Law of Moses itself that was "nailed to the cross." Yet, there is no reason to assume this, much less prove it. The Law only pertained to Jews (Israelites), not to Gentiles. Paul is not explaining what happened on behalf of Jews, but what Jesus did for *everyone* who was "dead" in their sins *and* "the uncircumcision of your flesh" (2:13)—i.e., specifically, Gentiles. If Jesus died for the whole world (John 3:16, 1 John 2:2), then His death was equally advantageous for Jews as well as Gentiles. Besides this, Jesus spoke of fulfilling the Law, not nailing it to His cross (or, putting it to death). Christ was put to death, not the Law; likewise, when we "die" with Christ, *we* are put to death, not sin itself (nor the laws that condemn us *of* sin). Through His death, the Law was fulfilled, *and* atonement was made possible for every sinner. Thus, what is actually "nailed to the cross" is God's condemnation against us for having trespassed His laws; Paul characterizes this condemnation as a written document.

is based upon a Greek word that describes the washing of ink from a papyrus, thus effectively removing the record of any debts written upon it (as in Acts 3:19).[156] This figurative washing is twofold for the believer: first, the record of his sins is "washed" away by the atoning blood of Christ; second, he himself is "washed" in a symbolic, born–again process (compare Acts 22:16 and 1 Peter 3:21). Another figure Paul employs here is that of "nailing" the certificate of death to the cross as a means of canceling it. "One ancient method of canceling bonds was to strike a nail through the writing."[157]

There has been centuries–long debate over exactly *what* was "nailed … to the cross": was it the Law of Moses itself? Or was it the spiritual debt or curse that *violating* the Law (or any of God's laws) created? If we say that Christ nailed the Law of Moses to the cross, this makes it look like the Law itself was the problem, and that Jesus came to remove it. This transfers the problem from the *sinner* to what God *provided* him, which skews Paul's words. Yet Paul says elsewhere that "the Law is holy, and the commandment is holy and righteous and good" (Rom. 7:12). And Jesus came to *fulfill* the Law of Moses (Mat. 5:17–18), not terminate it— certainly not to kill it (by nailing *it* to the cross). The cause of spiritual death is not the laws of God; it is the *violation* of such laws. This is what Paul says in 1 Cor. 15:56: "The sting of death is sin, and the power of sin is the law … ." The "sting" is divine condemnation for having violated the law; it is not the law that is sin, but the "power of sin" comes through violation of law. Thus, the *sinner* gives power to sin when *he* commits it. The debt he creates by *having* committed sin—i.e., God's condemnation of him—is what is nailed to the cross, not the law he violated. God's law is not cursed, but human souls are cursed for having sinned against it.

"[W]hen He disarmed the rulers and authorities … " (2:15)—a reference to Jesus' authority over those who supposed that *they* exercised

---

156 Robertson, *Word Pictures*, 493.

157 JFB, *Commentary* (electronic), on 2:14. As stated in the previous footnote, the "certificate" here is God's pronouncement of condemnation against the sinner, not the Law of Moses.

control over *Him* (John 11:47–53, 19:10–11).[158] The facts are otherwise: Jesus orchestrated the very events that led to His own sacrificial death and exercised complete mastery over the occasion of His arrest, trials, and crucifixion. The entire event was foreknown and prearranged. This does not remove the freewill of those involved; rather, it demonstrates the omniscience and omnipotence of God over all human effort and interference. God foreknew that if He sent His Son to *those particular people* at *that particular time* and at *that particular place,* the result would be His crucifixion. God's role of prearrangement was to bring all these conditions together, not to override the hearts of the ones who crucified His Son.

After Christ's resurrection, and as the gospel began to be proclaimed, it became clear that the rulers and authorities were clueless as to their assessment of who Christ was and what He came to do (see Acts 2:22–23, 3:17–18, and 1 Cor. 2:6–9, for example). Thus, Jesus proved Himself innocent to those who accused Him of being worthy of death. In effect, He exposed them as being wicked and/or ignorant while at the same time vindicated Himself through His self-resurrection from the dead.

---

158 Hendriksen, for one, believes these rulers and authorities to be Satan and his angels (*NTC*, 122–123). There is no question that Jesus bound the "strong man" (Mat. 12:29), and that this specifically refers to Satan; there is also no question that Satan was the prime motivator behind those who put Jesus on the cross. In the end, however, it does not seem necessary to separate the defeat of Satan from the defeat of those who allied themselves with him, with respect to those directly responsible for Jesus' crucifixion. Jesus overcame all His enemies, both physical and spiritual, in His resurrection from the dead.

Warnings against Self-imposed Religion (Col. 2:16–23)

"Therefore ... " (2:16)—what follows is based upon the foregoing text. This means:

- The believer has been forgiven of his sins "in Him" (1:13–14).
- Christ has all power and authority over anything that has begun to exist (1:15–17); even while He was on earth, the fullness of God dwelt within Him (2:9).
- Christ is the "head" of His church, which is His "body" (1:18).
- Christ prepares the believer to stand righteously before His Father (1:21–22).
- The believer has been "made complete" in Christ (1:28, 2:10).
- In baptism, Christ circumcises the believer with a spiritual circumcision that cannot be performed by men (2:11).
- Through the symbolic rite of baptism, the believer has put to death his old self and has been reborn (or, raised from his death) by Christ's power and authority (2:12).
- The decree that spelled spiritual death to the believer has been removed by his appeal to Christ's redemptive work on the cross (2:13–14).
- Even in His death, Christ showed mastery over everyone involved in it, proving His own innocence, *and* vindicating His every word to be true (2:15).

In other words, if one is "in Christ," there is no need for him to be "in" anything else, since Christ is everything he needs to stand complete before God. Furthermore, there is no need for him to follow the commands, convictions, or decrees of mere men, since no man has authority over another man's soul; and no man can impose his personal beliefs upon a servant of God (Rom. 14:4–8, 1 Cor. 7:23). (These refer to commands dealing with one's relationship with God, not commands concerning employment, law, government, etc.) These latter conclusions are the subject of Paul's letter from here to the end of chapter 2.

Shadows and Substance (2:16–17): "[N]o one is to act as your judge … " (2:16)—i.e., since Christ is the head of His church, and all who are "in Christ" are equals (Gal. 3:28), no believer has the right to dictate the beliefs or lifestyle of another. "Judge" here implies one who not only imposes his "law" upon another but also condemns the person who does not comply with it (as in Mat. 7:1–2 and James 4:11–12). Yet, no one has the right to sit on God's throne and pronounce either salvation or condemnation upon another by his own authority. The particulars that Paul cites here—food, drink, festivals, new moon, and Sabbath day—all refer to dietary restrictions, ritual feasts, or ordinances of the Law of Moses.[159] In other words, he refers to Judaizing teachers who impose requirements of the Law upon Gentile Christians. These things *were* important for the purpose they once served, but that purpose has been fulfilled in Christ and thus they are no longer necessary.[160] Such things were mere "shadows" of what was superior and enduring (2:17; see Heb. 10:1); no one is to follow the *shadow* once he has been shown the *substance* that created it. By following mere shadows, people reveal their ignorance of (or lack of concern for) the true substance of the Christian faith, which is not ritual observances or holy days but Christ Himself. The Levitical priesthood, sacrificial offerings, temple services, and all the ordinances of the Law itself pointed forward and prophesied of Christ.[161] To cling to the prophecies rather than the One who has fulfilled them is an approach that is both backward and inferior. Paul speaks forcefully

---

159 "Festival" refers to one of the three yearly observances required by the Law (Passover, Pentecost, and Feast of Booths). "New moon" refers to the monthly observance of the new moon, accompanied by sacrifices (Num. 10:10, 28:11–15). "Sabbath" refers to the weekly observance of the seventh day of the week, the completion of a full cycle of days (Exod. 20:8–11). Thus, Paul cites yearly, monthly, and weekly observances.

160 "No longer necessary" means that they are no longer *binding*, not that they are entirely useless to us. All that has been written and preserved in the OT serves to bring us to a better understanding of Christ and His redemptive work, as well as provide moral lessons concerning man's relationship to God (Rom. 15:4, 1 Cor. 10:11, etc.). Those who practically disregard the OT because it is "ancient history" or because it has been superseded by the gospel simply do not understand the wealth of knowledge and perspective that is contained in that sacred record.

161 This is at least what Christ meant in John 5:46: Moses "wrote about" Him in the details of the Law that prefigured the redemptive work of the world's Redeemer.

and directly against any such thinking.[162]

Seeking Completion Outside of Christ Is Useless (2:18–23): Having spoken positively about Christ and how He is the believer's completion, Paul now speaks against other alleged sources of completion (2:18–19). Apparently, some men are imposing upon the Colossians to accept parallel forms of worship. "Self-abasement" is a form of asceticism in which a person inflicts hardship or deprivation upon himself as a means of forced humility and drawing near to God. Similarly, in the case of angels, some believe that one's humility before God is so great that he needs to make appeals to Him through angels rather than praying to Him directly.[163] Likewise, "visions" indicates that, because some had seen special revelations from God, therefore these revelations themselves are considered a route to deeper piety ("I know what I saw—

---

162 The Epistle to the Hebrews is one grand sermon underscoring this point. I recommend my *Hebrews Commentary* (Spiritbuilding Publishers, 2011) for a much deeper study on this point; go to www.spiritbuilding.com/chad.

163 "In this teaching a decisive place was accorded to the angelic beings through whom the law was given [Gal. 3:19, Heb. 2:2, etc.]. They were not only elemental spirits but dominant ones as well—principalities and powers, lords of the planetary spheres, sharers in the plenitude of the divine essence. Since [according to Jewish angelology] they controlled the lines of communication between God and man, all revelation from God to man and all prayer and thought wise to cultivate their good will and pay them such homage as they desired. Moreover, since they were the agents through whom the divine law was given, the keeping of the law [of Moses] was regarded as a tribute of obedience to them, and the breaking of the law incurred their displeasure and brought the law-breaker into debt and bondage to them. Hence they must be placated, not only by the regular legal observances of traditional Judaism—circumcision, the sabbath and the various sacred seasons of the Levitical year, food restrictions and so forth—but by a rigorous asceticism" (Bruce, "Commentary," 167; bracketed words are mine). Yet "Scripture clearly opposes the idea of 'patrons' or 'intercessors' (1 Tim. 2:5–6). True Christian humility comes from realizing that our only worth is due to Christ's intervention on our behalf" (JFB, *Commentary* [electronic], on 2:18). See similar thoughts in Coffman (*Commentary*, 388, 390–391) and Hendriksen (*NTC*, 126). Lenski, on the other hand, sees the phrase "worship of the angels" as *not* being one person's worship *of* an angel, but imitating the kind of solemn and reverent worship that angels *give* to God (*Interpretation*, 132). This, however, begs the question: what other kind of worship attitude *ought* we to have? If angels teach us anything, it is how to conduct ourselves in God's presence; certainly, Paul would not have dissuaded us from learning this lesson. Thus, the first interpretation seems to be more accurate because it is the most natural and relevant.

God *showed* it to me specially!").

In each case, the worshiper indirectly draws attention to himself by emphasizing his personal humility, and the one who trains him to do so delights in his control over this person. Paul states that such beliefs or practices are useless in seeking fellowship with God. Instead, the believer is to "[hold] fast to the head" of the body—in other words, he is to cling tenaciously to Christ rather than anything or anyone else. From the head comes all the wisdom and instruction that is necessary for the body to operate properly. The ligaments and joints of the body connect every member together, so that the head can communicate its will to every part of the body. So it is with the church: Christ is the head that controls His spiritual body of believers; there is no need for another source of wisdom or instruction. Being connected to the head (Christ) provides for "a growth which is from God" rather than the semblance of growth which is man–made or self–determined (cf. Eph. 4:15–16).

Paul then poses a rhetorical question to the Colossians (2:20–22). "If you have died" really means "*Since* you have died," because no one can become a Christian without uniting with Christ in the likeness of His death (Rom. 6:3–5). One's burial in water in his baptism symbolizes this "death" (recall 2:11–12). And, since this is true that the Christian has given full allegiance to Christ (having died to all other allegiances), it is impossible for him to give equal allegiance to "elementary principles of the world."[164]

The "decrees" mentioned here are not instructions from God (such as, "Do not drink blood"—Acts 15:29) but are human decrees or traditions forced upon believers and considered on par with the laws of God (i.e., the "commandments and teachings of men"—see Mat. 15:1–9). These decrees intended to bring the believer away from his contact with the world to draw closer to heaven. The *problem*, however, is the emphasis on personal righteousness (or justification) rather than seeking righteousness through Christ. In other words, this other approach is an inferior and worldly repackaging of the Christian lifestyle. It promotes a

---

[164] Concerning the word "elementary" [Greek *stoicheion*], see notes on 2:8.

salvation–by–works theology that denies the power of divine grace (Gal. 5:1–4). Furthermore, one cannot find heavenly completion through things which belong to this transient world (or that will "perish"—see 1 John 2:16–17).

Since the church began, men have tried to improve upon God's system of salvation by adding to it their own systems of righteousness and personal piety. Such alleged improvements "have … the appearance of wisdom," but are the products of self–made religion and are unable to compare to God's gospel of grace (2:23).[165] Human–designed salvation is really no salvation at all; asceticism ("self–abasement and severe treatment of the body") is not the means by which a person overcomes spiritual temptations or brings about moral purity; "Neglect of the body will never cure the soul."[166] Only by clinging to Christ and following God's Holy Spirit can a person truly draw near to God and overcome the effects of this world upon the human soul. All other attempts or so–called solutions are hopelessly dependent upon flawless human behavior, which is impossible to produce. If Christ is who completes us, then we cannot become *more* complete in something less than Him. To teach otherwise is illogical as well as unbiblical.

---

165 Where NASB has "self–made religion," KJV has "will worship"—i.e., a worship of God created by one's own effort, imagination, and determination. In effect, the creature (human being) chooses to worship his Creator (God) in whatever way pleases *him* rather than seeking to please *God*.

166 Hendriksen, *NTC*, 133.

The Transcendent Christian Perspective
(Col. 3:1–4)

Seeking the Things Above (3:1–2): Having dealt with the external pressures to conform to man–made teachings, Paul now turns to the inward transformation that is expected in the one who belongs to Christ (3:1). "If you have been raised up" means "*Since* you have been raised up": the situation is conditional (an "If … then" clause), but in the case of the Colossian Christians, this condition has been satisfied. All Christians *became* Christians through a symbolic resurrection from the watery grave of baptism (Rom. 6:3–5). "[K]eep seeking the things above" indicates an ongoing and active process rather than limiting it to a historical event in the past. The believer once sought God by calling upon His name for salvation; now as a Christian he is to continue seeking Him in faith (Heb. 11:6). The "things above" indicates those things (or truths) that are far superior to the things of the world below (see James 3:13–18 for a contrast of these two realms). In other words, rather than seeking completion in the things *below*, one should strive to seek completion in the things *above*, which transcend the created world.

There is no higher authority (outside of the Father's own authority) than to be "seated at the right hand of God" (3:1). Since antiquity, the "right hand" has been a symbol of power and pre-eminence. To sit at the king's right hand indicates a position of power and glory second only to the king himself (cf. Gen. 41:39–44). This is the position that Christ holds in heaven: He is above all that He has created, and only the Father Himself is exempted from His power (1 Cor. 15:27–28). Consider the several passages that speak of this (all bracketed words are mine):

- "He [Jesus] said to them, 'Then how does David in the Spirit call Him "Lord," saying, "The Lord said to my Lord, 'Sit at My right hand, until I put Your enemies beneath Your feet'"?" (Mat. 22:43–44).
- "So then, when the Lord Jesus had spoken to them, He was received up into heaven and sat down at the right hand of God" (Mark

16:19).
- "But from now on the Son of Man will be seated at the right hand of the power of God" (Luke 22:69).
- "Therefore having been exalted to the right hand of God, and having received from the Father the promise of the Holy Spirit, He has poured forth this which you both see and hear" (Acts 2:33).
- "He is the one whom God exalted to His right hand as a Prince and a Savior, to grant repentance to Israel, and forgiveness of sins" (Acts 5:31).
- "But being full of the Holy Spirit, he [Stephen] gazed intently into heaven and saw the glory of God, and Jesus standing at the right hand of God … " (Acts 7:55).
- " … Christ Jesus is He who died, yes, rather who was raised, who is at the right hand of God, who also intercedes for us" (Rom. 8:34).
- "These [riches] are in accordance with the working of the strength of His might which He brought about in Christ, when He raised Him from the dead and seated Him at His right hand in the heavenly places, far above all rule and authority and power and dominion, and every name that is named, not only in this age but also in the one to come" (Eph. 1:19–21).
- " … When He had made purification of sins, He sat down at the right hand of the Majesty on high, having become as much better than the angels … " (Heb. 1:3–4).
- "Now the main point in what has been said is this: we have such a high priest, who has taken His seat at the right hand of the throne of the Majesty in the heavens … " (Heb. 8:1).
- " … But He, having offered one sacrifice for sins for all time, sat down at the right hand of God … " (Heb. 10:12).
- " … Fixing our eyes on Jesus, the author and perfecter of faith, who for the joy set before Him endured the cross, despising the shame, and has sat down at the right hand of the throne of God" (Heb. 12:2).
- "[Christ] is at the right hand of God, having gone into heaven, after angels and authorities and powers had been subjected to Him" (1 Peter 3:22).

This is a substantial list of references. Christ, entrusted with kingship over His Father's entire kingdom, has been given all authority, all rule, and all power over all Creation. God has also given Him headship over the church (recall 1:15–18). There is no need for secondary or supplemental powers or authorities; Christ has no rivals, competition, or challengers to His throne. This is the message Paul communicates to the church in this passage (3:1). While the believer no longer lives to the world, he is made alive through the power of the One who reigns over it.

Since Christ is at the right hand of God and is the object of our faith, this is where we must place our rapt attention (3:2). To "set your mind [or, be intent on]" indicates a personal and deliberate decision (as in Mat. 6:33), not an automatic or reflexive one. It also indicates an internal focus despite whatever external troubles or conflicts might be present. Christ's love, power, and holiness draw us to Him; our faith in Him draws Him to us. "For you have died … " (3:3)—to become a Christian, one must "die" to his old self and be re–born ("born again") as a child of God (John 3:5, 2 Tim. 2:11, and 1 Peter 1:3).[167] This spiritual rebirth also recalibrates our thinking, perspective, and conduct differently than those who still remain in the old creation (i.e., having been born of blood, the will of the flesh, and the will of man—John 1:12–13).

A Life Hidden in Christ (3:3–4): While we remain visible to the world, our spiritual union with Christ is (for now) invisible, since we have not yet seen it fully realized. Thus, our life with Christ in God is "hidden" (3:3), even though it is real and functional and not imaginary or wishful. Our spiritual life is hidden for now, but it will not always be so: "When Christ … is revealed" (3:4), our life with Him will also be fully revealed "in glory." This revealing cannot be anything other than the Second Coming of Christ. Consider other passages that correspond to this (bracketed words are mine):

---

167 Incidentally, the phrase "born-again Christian" is redundant. No one is a Christian who has not been "born again"; likewise, all who *are* "born again" are also known as Christians. There is no other *kind* of Christian than one who has undergone this born–again process.

- "[You are] awaiting eagerly the revelation of our Lord Jesus Christ, who will also confirm you to the end, blameless in the day of our Lord Jesus Christ" (1 Cor. 1:7–8).
- "But each [will be raised] in his own order: Christ the first fruits, after that those who are Christ's at His coming … " (1 Cor. 15:23).
- "For who is our hope or joy or crown of exultation? Is it not even you, in the presence of our Lord Jesus at His coming?" (1 Thess. 2:19).
- " … so that He may establish your hearts without blame in holiness before our God and Father at the coming of our Lord Jesus with all His saints" (1 Thess. 3:13).
- "For the Lord Himself will descend from heaven with a shout, with the voice of the archangel and with the trumpet of God … " (1 Thess. 4:16).
- "Now may the God of peace Himself sanctify you entirely; and may your spirit and soul and body be preserved complete, without blame at the coming of our Lord Jesus Christ" (1 Thess. 5:23).
- " … the Lord Jesus will be revealed from heaven with His mighty angels in flaming fire, dealing out retribution to those who do not know God and to those who do not obey the gospel of our Lord Jesus. These will pay the penalty of eternal destruction, away from the presence of the Lord and from the glory of His power, when He comes to be glorified in His saints on that day, and to be marveled at among all who have believed … " (2 Thess. 1:7–10).
- "[I charge you to] keep the commandment without stain or reproach until the appearing of our Lord Jesus Christ … " (1 Tim. 6:14).
- "[We are] looking for the blessed hope and the appearing of the glory of our great God and Savior, Christ Jesus … " (Titus 2:13).
- "[You] are protected by the power of God through faith for a salvation ready to be revealed in the last time … [and] may be found to result in praise and glory and honor at the revelation of Jesus Christ … " (1 Peter 1:5, 7).
- "Therefore, prepare your minds for action, keep sober in spirit, fix your hope completely on the grace to be brought to you at the revelation of Jesus Christ" (1 Peter 1:13).
- " … But to the degree that you share the sufferings of Christ, keep

on rejoicing, so that also at the revelation of His glory you may rejoice with exultation" (1 Peter 4:13).
- ❑ "Now, little children, abide in Him, so that when He appears, we may have confidence and not shrink away from Him in shame at His coming" (1 John 2:28).

In a future day, Christ will reveal Himself in glory to the entire world. For those who belong to Him, this will be a day of triumph and divine vindication; for those who do not belong to Him, this will be a day of divine wrath and vengeance. He will glorify those who belong to Him and they will join Him and His throng of angels; "and so we shall always be with the Lord" (1 Thess. 4:17). This is the Christian's hope, but it is not a weak or wishful one. As real as Christ's Coming will be, so will be our future glory with Him. Yet this is contingent on our seeking the things above and keeping our eyes fixed upon Him (Heb. 12:1–2).

The "New Self"
(Col. 3:5–11)

Bringing One's Body in Subjection to Christ (3:5–7): If the believer has died to the world and now lives to God in Christ, then it makes sense that "the members of your earthly body" must conform to this great transition (3:5). "Members" is not figurative language but refers to the believer's actual body that is under the control of his head (or heart).[168] Just as Jesus is the head of His church, and the church is thus to conform to the will of the head, so the body of the believer is to conform to the converted and transformed heart of the believer (Rom. 6:11–13).

This conformity is not automatic, however. The body has a physical connection to this world and is conditioned by its wicked influences, carnal appetites, and satanic desires. This creates an inevitable conflict and persistent tension between the spiritual believer in Christ and his physical presence in the natural world. These two natures are not merely incompatible but are antagonistic toward each other (Gal. 5:16–17). While the members of one's body are to be regarded as "dead" to sin, worldly desires and sinful cravings (immorality, impurity, passion, etc.[169]) continue to exert their pull and influence on the believer's heart. While one cannot put these desires or forces to death in the entire world, he can and *must* put them to death within himself (Rom. 8:12–14).[170]

This means all Christians are consciously to suppress these wicked desires from influencing our heart *and at the same time* choosing to fill

---

168 "The 'body' is here viewed as the instrument by which all the sins of the heart become realities in the outward life. The 'body' itself is the seat of the lower appetites and is called 'mortal.' Paul probably uses this term to remind us of how unsuitable this reign of sin is in those who are 'alive from the dead'" (JFB, *Commentary* [electronic], on Rom. 6:12).

169 For an exposition on these words, see my *Galatians and Ephesians Commentary* (Spiritbuilding Publishers, 2012) on Gal. 5:19–21 and Eph. 5:3–5; go to www.spiritbuilding.com/chad.

170 "John Calvin may be on the right track when he states that these *vices* are called *members* 'since they adhere so closely to us'" (Hendriksen, *NTC*, 145). This seems also to be Jesus' meaning in Mat. 5:29–30.

our mind with the things of God instead (Phil. 4:8–9). "Greed" and "idolatry" (3:5) go together, since one's god becomes that for which his heart is greedy. One who belongs to God in Christ has no business giving attention to any other god (or, object of worship). This other god can be in the form of a lifestyle, behavior, belief, spouse, child(ren), male or female human being, or anything or person that reigns over a person's heart. "A man really worships that on which his heart is set, which is the chief end of his labor in life. That which man most ardently desires, he worships; and the service he renders in obtaining it is worship."[171]

"[T]hese things" (3:6)—namely, immorality, impurity, etc.—stand opposed to God and therefore incite His holy wrath (cf. Rom. 1:18–20). This "wrath of God" refers to divine anger (or vengeance) that will consume those who defiantly oppose the very source of their own existence. Such wrath is not merely the *separation* from God, but also necessarily implies His divine *punishment*. It is true that those who experience His wrath will be separated from Him; it is also true that those who are thus separated will consciously experience divine punishment in their separation.

"[S]ons of disobedience" (3:6) are in direct contrast to "sons of God" (Gal. 3:26) and "children of light" (Eph. 5:8). Such people are not predestined to be disobedient (as if against their own free will) but have chosen this course through their rejection of God. Likewise, no one becomes a son of God or child of light apart from his own decision to pursue this. "[A]nd in them you also once walked … " (3:7)—i.e., because you (Christians) were once sons of disobedience, you also incurred God's wrath (Titus 3:3). "Walked" indicates one's daily conduct; "living" implies the pattern that dictates this walk. Believers had to come out of the sinful world to walk with God: only by separating themselves *from* the world can they be separated *to* God (2 Cor. 6:16–18).

Putting on the New Self (3:8–11): "But now … put them all aside" (3:8)—"them" referring to the behaviors mentioned in 3:5, as well as

---

[171] Lipscomb, *Commentary*, 292.

those he now mentions: anger, wrath, malice, slander, etc.[172] These things reveal the god that is being served: not the God of heaven, but the god of this world (2 Cor. 4:3–4). Such a character is satanic or demonic in nature, as well as self-serving and self-ambitious (James 3:15–16). People led by Satan also act and speak like him; those led by Christ will act and speak like *Him*. The fact that we can put satanic behavior "all aside" necessarily implies that we have control over—and thus are responsible for—our conduct. Paul is not accusing the Colossians of engaging in these things, but he is saying that such conduct is incompatible with their walk in Christ.

"Do not lie [or, Stop lying] to one another … " (3:9)—lying, in any form (deception, evasion, distortion of the facts, etc.), is evidence of one's having given himself over to a wicked influence. This kind of behavior has no place in the new self (3:9–10). The "old self" was "laid aside" (as though in a grave) in baptism; it has no right to exercise control over the Christian. Having died to sin, the believer also died to its mastery over him. Nonetheless, if he chooses to dabble in the sins in which he once lived, then those evil influences will *control* him rather than be "laid aside" *by* him. Being dead to the world and alive to Christ does not refer only to one's conversion experience. In sharp contrast to the "old self," the "new self" (3:10) is in a constant state of renewal and reflects the very nature of God Himself. (This "new self" is an individual person, whereas the "new man" in Eph. 2:15 is the entire church of Christ. Nonetheless, the *nature* and *character* of both must be consistent.) This "new self" enjoys the "true knowledge" that God has revealed—that which is not only *known* but also practiced in a visible manner. There is a very real sense of a *new creation* here, as though the physical Creation is spiritually replicated in the life of each believer. The Creator in both cases remains the same: the Christ who has created the physical world (recall 1:15–17) is He who gives life to the "new creation" in Him (2 Cor. 5:17). While the physical world has been irreparably corrupted and lies under a curse, the believer basks in the glory of his Creator and lives according to the promise of an inheritance in light

---

172 For an exposition on these words, see my *Galatians and Ephesians Commentary* on Eph. 4:29–31.

(recall 1:12). Thus, the believer is indeed "Christ-like"—a *Christian*. In this "renewal" (or spiritual regeneration), all physical, ethnic, national, and former religious distinctions are irrelevant (3:11).[173] Likewise, all social statuses are meaningless, such as the status of a slave or a free man. This does *not* mean these distinctions are no longer in existence, since most of these cannot be changed, but that *in Christ* they have no purpose. Christ's body is a singular, unified, and interrelated assemblage of believers who all have the same mind, are led by the same Spirit, and answer to the same head. While this oneness is spiritual in nature, it must also bear directly on how we regard one another and thus treat one another (Phil. 2:3–5). "[B]ut Christ is all, and is in all"—i.e., just as Christ holds the physical world together by His own power and authority, so He unites the spiritual church into one cohesive body. Thus, no one who is "in Christ" can legitimately hold another who is "in Christ" in contempt. This thought leads into the next section, where Paul describes how those in Christ are to regard and treat one another.

---

[173] "Barbarian" refers to a person who is not born into or taught according to a Greek–influenced society. In other words, it is one who is regarded as an uncivilized or uncultured person. "Scythian" refers to those regarded as savages who lived north of the Black Sea and Caucasus Mountains; they are related to the Parthians of warring fame. According to the Greek historian Herodotus, they were nomadic, filthy, drank the blood of their enemies, and made bowls from the skulls of those whom they had killed (H. Porter, "Scythians," *ISBE* [electronic]). How much of this is true and how much of this is the result of myths, legends, and folklore will never be known for certain. However, it is true that these people became a scourge against the Roman Empire for many years. Paul's point is not to single out these people, but to use them as an example: if (even) a Scythian is in Christ, then he is no *less* a Christian than anyone else in Christ. "Since the Scythian invasion of the 'Fertile Crescent' [i.e., Mesopotamia] towards the end of the seventh century BC, these people's name had become a byword for uncultured barbarians" (Bruce, *Commentary*, 276, bracketed word is mine).

Results of the Transformed Life
(Col. 3:12–17)

Those who identify with God (in Christ) must conduct themselves accordingly. There is no excuse for improper, ungodly, or illicit behavior; on the contrary, we are to live to a much higher standard than that of the unconverted world (3:12). Christians are "chosen of God"—i.e., they belong to the church that has been predestined for glory (cf. Rom. 8:29–30 and Eph. 1:3–5).[174] This group is "holy and beloved": "holy" refers to its conformity to the nature of God; "beloved" refers to the intimate relationship it has with Him.

What Christians Are to Put on (3:12–14): "[P]ut on a heart of compassion, etc."—earlier (recall 3:5, 8, and 9), the Colossian Christians were told to "put aside" or "lay aside" their worldly thinking and behavior; here, they are told to "put on" something. In every case where the word of God instructs Christians to put *off* one thing, it also teaches us to put *on* something else (cf. Titus 2:11–12). The things we are to "put on" (3:12) begin as attitudes of the heart but ultimately and necessarily must become our visible conduct.[175] They describe the gentle and humble disposition of Christ (Mat. 11:29) and are the opposite of anger, wrath, malice, slander, and abusive speech that Paul mentioned earlier (recall 3:8).

"[B]earing with ... and forgiving each other" (3:13)—i.e., exhibiting a desire for *reconciliation* and *restoration* rather than separation

---

174 Paul's use of "chosen" or "predestined" indicates a *collective* or *corporate* sense, not an individual one. In other words, the *church* has been predestined to be the recipient of God's divine blessings; but no single *person* has been so predestined against his own will, as Calvinism teaches. Whether one becomes a part of this chosen group of people is dependent upon (or, conditioned by) his personal faith in Christ; regardless, the church remains a chosen group with or without each person's choice to identify with it. We cannot confuse one's *choice* to be saved with the *power* that is required to save him. No one is saved only because of his choice; however, anyone who deliberately calls upon the name of the Lord will be saved by Him (Rom. 10:11–17).

175 For an exposition on these words, see my *Galatians and Ephesians Commentary* on Gal. 5:22–23 and Eph. 4:1–3.

and condemnation. Forbearance describes one's patience toward another person's inexperienced, immature, or unintentional conduct. Forgiveness refers to the proper dealing of a person's past offenses or sins. The first deals with unwise choices; the second, with definable sins against another person—and thus, against Christ. We are never told to be forbearing toward sin, and we are never told to forgive what is merely a matter of poor judgment.[176] Lipscomb summarizes: "In differences in which we feel that we are right and our brethren are wrong, we should be gentle and patient, not quick to assert our rights, or to avenge the wrongs others committed against us."[177]

"[J]ust as the Lord forgave you … "—i.e., those chosen of God are to imitate the same kind of mercy and forgiveness Christ has already shown to them (Rom. 15:7). One who refuses to forgive his brother also refuses to show love to him; one who will not love his brother in Christ has no fellowship with God (see 1 John 2:9–10 and 4:19–21).[178] This is essentially a recap of what Jesus had already stated in His sermon on the mount (Mat. 6:14–15). All these virtues are bound together by God's love for His church and the believer's love for God (3:14). This "perfect bond of unity" is linked to the "unity of the Spirit in the bond of peace" (Eph. 4:3). Peace and fellowship with God's Spirit are visibly reflected in the Christian's virtuous treatment of his brothers and sisters in Christ.

What Is to Rule and Fill Our Hearts (3:15–17): Instead of being led or driven by self-serving and satanic impulses of the world, the believer is to be controlled by Christ (3:15). The word "let" (in 3:15 and 3:16) indicates that one's personal decision to comply with this instruction will be consistent with God's expectation of him. The peace He brings to the believer's heart, and the resulting peace that the believer himself

---

176 For a deeper study of "forgiveness," I strongly recommend my book, *The Gospel of Forgiveness* (Spiritbuilding Publishers, 2016); go to www.spiritbuilding.com/chad.

177 Lipscomb, *Commentary*, 296.

178 This point necessarily implies that the *conditions* for forgiveness have been met. We cannot forgive someone who will not take responsibility for and repent of his sins; yet if these conditions *are* met, we have no good reason to withhold forgiveness. For a far deeper study on this subject, I recommend my book, *The Gospel of Forgiveness* (Spiritbuilding Publishers, 2011); go to www.spiritbuilding.com/chad.

pursues with others, mirrors the peace that exists between Christ and His Father (cf. John 17:20–22). "Rule" is taken from a Greek word which means "to act as an umpire" or "to arbitrate."[179] Thus, when the believer feels tempted to respond in the manner of the world, this peace restrains him from pursuing such passions. This peace characterizes the church's holy fellowship with Christ, so it is only right that each member should allow it to rule over him. "[A]nd be thankful"—those who are at peace with God will respond with thankfulness; those who are ungrateful for or indifferent toward the salvation He offers are not at peace with Him.

"Let the word of Christ richly dwell within you … " (3:16). The internalization of the gospel of Christ ought to reveal itself in one's personal conduct *toward* others and his songs of praise *with* others. "Psalms" refer to poems or odes set to music; "hymns" refer specifically to sacred songs in praise of God; "spiritual songs" are all religious songs used as a form of worship *and* that provide teaching about God to one another. "Singing" is the form of teaching and admonishing that Paul instructs here. Thus, these songs are not for entertainment or to highlight the vocal talents of select individuals. Rather, they serve a purpose like that of preaching and the exposition of God's word. These songs do not communicate mere music, but also teaching and admonition.

Music is the vehicle here, not the objective; educating and encouraging the church *and* honoring God are the objectives. Singing is a unique form of collective activity among the saints that allows for *many* voices to be joined into *one* voice (or song). The blending of various voices (and the various ages, talents, statuses, etc. of those who give them) illustrates the kind of unity and fellowship that is to be exercised within the church in all other areas. These songs are not sung *to* fellow believers (as though from a choir) but are to be sung *by* all believers.

Today, most congregational vocal singing has been either overtaken or altogether replaced by instrumental music—an impossible position to maintain from what Paul teaches here. Edification and admonition are

---

179 Thayer, *Lexicon* (electronic), G1018.

no longer objectives, but entertainment and personal enjoyment reign supreme. Churches that use instrumental music (especially, that employ a band to provide their music) will all claim to be worshiping God, but true worship (John 4:24) is not to be determined by the preferences of the worshipers but the One being worshiped.[180]

Singing is a form of worship to God ("singing with thankfulness in your hearts to God") as well as means of collective fellowship with His church. "Whatever you do ... , do all in the name of the Lord Jesus" (3:17)—a general instruction that applies across the board to every activity, whether in the context of spiritual worship or in everyday conduct. To do something in Jesus' name means to follow His word, His character, and His regard for those who belong to Him (see 1 John 2:6). "[I]n the name of the Lord" defers to His authority rather than one's own; the believer seeks His approval over that of anyone else. Again, gratitude ("giving thanks") must be an ingredient in one's devotion to Christ. "The first human motive in the Christian life is gratitude for redemption, and it does not lose its power as we feel more and more how great a Redeemer the Lord Jesus is."[181]

---

180 For comments regarding *a capella* singing versus the use of musical instruments, see my *Galatians and Ephesians Study Workbook* on Eph. 5:19.
181 Lipscomb, *Commentary*, 301.

Relationships in the Lord
(Col. 3:18—4:1)

Having spoken all Christians in general, Paul now turns his attention to specific roles typically found in any congregation: spouses, children, fathers, slaves, and masters. This is hardly a comprehensive coverage on any one role and is briefer than parallel instructions in *Ephesians*.[182] The purpose here is not to belabor the point but to provide practical application of the general truths he has already discussed. If the believer has his heart fixed upon Christ, who sits at the right hand of God (recall 3:1), he (or she) must reflect that attitude in his behavior toward his wife (or husband), in the family, and in his occupation. In other words, the Christian belief system is not limited to the context of worship services, church functions, or the company of fellow believers. It extends into and permeates all realms of one's life, however secular or non-spiritual they may seem otherwise. Since Christ has purchased us with His blood, He owns us entirely—we are His possession (1 Cor. 6:19-20). This means He owns every part of us and every aspect of our lives, and thus governs every relationship to which we belong.

Instructions to Spouses (3:18-19): "Wives, be subject … as is fitting in the Lord" (3:18). A wife's subjection to her husband is not a separate matter from her subjection to Christ. Her spiritual subjection to the Lord *conditions* or *governs* her subjection to her husband. Subjection is not a demeaning evaluation of a person's worth; it is merely a comparison of one's rank (or position) to another's, as in the military. God has made the husband the head of the household; God expects the wife to honor and support her husband's position. The husband's position of authority in the home is over that of his wife's position. This does not make him a superior person, or his wife an inferior one, but simply recognizes the difference in roles or responsibilities that God has assigned to these two people. The phrase "in the Lord" means "what the

---

[182] See my *Galatians and Ephesians Commentary* (Spiritbuilding Publishers, 2012) on Eph. 5:22—6:9 for a much fuller exposition than is found here; go to www.spiritbuilding.com/chad.

Lord would approve of," exclusively for those who are "in Christ." "Husbands, love your wives ... " (3:19)—Paul does not direct this command to "love" *only* to husband (see Titus 2:4), but husbands should take the leadership role in demonstrating godly love in the marriage. Christ's love for His church must be the pattern for a husband's love for his wife (Eph. 5:25), which is selfless and sacrificial in nature. As with a wife's subjection, a husband's love for his wife is not a separate matter from his love for the Lord. His love for Christ ought to *condition* or *govern* his love for his wife. While the husband is the head of the marriage, love puts him in a servant role to his wife (just as Christ is also the head of His church yet serves His bride selflessly). "[A]nd do not be embittered against them"—i.e., do not be irritated with or indignant toward them. While love is selfless and noble, bitterness is selfish and worldly in nature. This does not mean a man can never be angry toward or upset with his wife (or vice versa), but that this reaction cannot serve as a ruling principle for his behavior and must not continue for long (Eph. 4:26).

Instructions Regarding Children (3:20–21): "Children, be obedient ... for this is well-pleasing to the Lord" (3:20). Are these children *Christians*, or merely children of Christian parents? Either scenario would apply equally, if they are still under the roof of their father's house. Clearly, Paul is not speaking of very young children (say, single-digit aged) but children who are old enough to be responsible for their behavior yet remain subject to their parents' oversight. (Adult children who no longer live with their parents cannot be obedient in this same context.) "Obedient" means following the rules (of the house) that do not conflict with the transcendent laws of God. God has always expected children to honor their parents (Exod. 20:12, Eph. 6:1–3), and for good reason: one's honor of his earthly source of life parallels the proper honor of his Creator. "Waves of lawlessness sweep over the world because the child was not taught to obey."[183]

"Fathers, do not exasperate your children ... " (3:21)—lit., do not infuriate, enrage, or overwhelm with frustration (Eph. 6:4). Fathers

---

183 Robertson, *Word Pictures*, 506.

have the responsibility to manage their household (1 Tim. 3:4–5), but this position can easily be abused or used in a self-serving manner. It is in the best interest of the children for fathers to lead them to the Lord, not incite anger, bitterness, or ill-feelings due to the father's poor representation of Him. Jesus declared that those who deliberately or carelessly drive their children away from the Lord will answer for this (Mat. 18:5–6, 10). This instruction is brief yet significant: the father's abuse of his authority or his perversion of justice (within the home) is a source of provocation for children. This would be the case if he:

- puts stumbling blocks in the (spiritual) path of his children (Mat. 18:6).
- fails to be consistent in the administration of rules, justice, rewards, or punishments.
- is a hypocrite—i.e., he portrays himself in one manner when with Christians, but in an entirely different manner when in the privacy of his home.
- makes no effort to live what he preaches to his children (Rom. 2:21–24).
- fails to prepare them for life, setting them up for future failure.
- is overprotective and does not allow his children the ability to exercise responsibility.
- is neglectful and gives little time or attention to his children.
- is abusive, either mentally or physically.

Instructions Regarding Slaves and Masters (3:22—4:1): The instructions for "slaves" are general ones that might be loosely applied to modern employees who work under a boss (or "master") in some company or corporation. In the ancient world, "slaves" had broad application, and not all slaves engaged in hard labor or dangerous occupations.[184] Many slaves were educated men who, because of

---

184 Some slave occupations were domestic (cooks, waiters, maids, seamstresses, costumers, bath attendants, etc.) Others were craftsmen (cobblers, blacksmiths, silversmiths, plumbers, masons, builders, etc.). Still others were trained as accountants, educators, physicians, midwives, or managers. Some slaves even owned property, ran schools, ran their own businesses, and had slaves of their own. Production slavery, however, had the worst of conditions. Slaves who worked in mines, quarries, farming,

circumstances beyond their control, found themselves under the authority of a master. Likewise, not all masters were the same: some were fair, decent, and humane; others were unjust, abusive, and crooked.[185] In any case, the Christian "slave" has a moral obligation to God to serve in a manner that rightly represents Him, even to his own hurt. This service is not to be good when "the boss" is looking but unproductive when he is not; rather, it is to be always good, regardless of who is watching. This is because *God* is always watching and expects His servants to be always consistent and honorable. The word "heartily" [lit., from the soul[186]] indicates that a Christian slave's *work* is to reflect the faithful disposition of his *heart*. Because he has devoted his heart to Christ, his work will demonstrate that devotion in his service to his earthly master.

"Whatever you do ... as for the Lord" (3:23) is a principle that extends well beyond the sphere of one's employment (although this is the immediate context in this passage). This means that even in times of rest or recreation, or in the company of friends, the Christian is to conduct himself in a manner that is consistent with his profession of faith in Christ. His spiritual inheritance depends upon the genuineness of his earthly conduct (2 Cor. 5:10). If he conducts himself well in this life, he will reap the benefits of this in the life to come; if he says one thing but does another, then he will reap the consequences of that duplicitous life (3:24–25; see Rom. 2:9–11). In other words, how a believer chooses to conduct himself in his earthly circumstances, regardless of how blessed or difficult those circumstances might be, directly impacts the "reward of [his] inheritance." "The reliance of the Christian, in whatever state of life, upon the eternal justice of God's universe is the great stabilizer of the human heart. Without this reliance, life becomes an idiot's dream where injustice, misery, caprice, chance and luck are supreme."[187]

and other intensely laborious contexts not only endured daily physical exhaustion but were given barely enough food to eat and clothing to stay warm. Not surprisingly, these slaves had short lifespans and had to be regularly replaced (Henry C. Boren, *Roman Society*, 2nd ed. [Lexington, MA: Heath and Co., 1992], 222–5).

185 See 1 Peter 2:18–20, where the Greek word for "unreasonable" [*skolios*] means crooked or morally perverse (Strong, *Dictionary* [electronic], G4646).

186 *Ibid.*, G5590.

187 Coffman, *Commentary*, 412.

"Masters, grant your slaves justice and fairness … " (4:1). The primary abuse among masters of slaves in the ancient world was that of injustice through an abuse of their authority. While Christian slaves are to be just in their service to their masters (whether these masters are believers), Christian masters are to be just in the treatment of their slaves (whether these slaves are believers). In the modern application, all Christians who are in positions of authority over others are to exercise that authority with a view to their spiritual relationship with God: "you too have a Master in heaven." From Christ's point–of–view, all believers are equal (Gal. 3:28); thus, we cannot allow our earthly circumstances to contradict or circumvent this spiritual perspective.

Section Four:
Final Remarks and Salutations (4:2–18)

What Is Expected of Believers
(Col. 4:2–6)

Instructions on Prayer (4:2–4): In this brief but potent section, Paul provides practical application of our holy union with God through Christ. This instruction is for all believers, regardless of earthly relationships or statuses. "Devote yourselves to prayer … " (4:2)—i.e., persevere in this; be earnestly committed to it. "[Paul] was not urging long prayers, but the continuance of the habit of prayer."[188] There is a difference between those who say prayers and those devoted to prayer. One person uses prayer as a means of appeasing his guilty conscience, or to "get things" that he does not have. Another person uses prayer as a means of holy and intimate communication with his Father—a communication that is as rewarding as it is necessary. "Keeping alert in it" implies a sense of diligent vigilance, or a sense of keen awareness to the need for continual communication with the Lord. This is the case not only when God grants prayerful petitions, but also when He denies them. Thus, the "attitude of thanksgiving" is not to be present only when God says "yes," but also when He says "no" or "wait." "The Christian is to be thankful for God's responses to himself and others, whether they seem to be pleasant or unpleasant at the time."[189]

Paul adds a personal addendum to this instruction: "praying at the same time for us as well" (4:3–4)—"us" meaning (at least) himself and Timothy (recall 1:1). Paul is still in Roman imprisonment at the time of this writing, limiting his opportunity to teach the gospel. Nonetheless, he still exerts a great amount of influence and provide apostolic direction despite his circumstances; "I suffer hardship even to imprisonment as a criminal; but the word of God is not imprisoned" (2 Tim. 2:9). Even though an inspired apostle, Paul consistently relies upon the prayers

---

188 Lipscomb, *Commentary*, 307.
189 JFB, *Commentary* (electronic), on 4:2.

of fellow believers for courage, opportunity, and success (Rom. 15:30, Eph. 6:18, etc.). In this case, Paul seeks an open "door" to teaching the word of God and the "mystery of Christ" (which elsewhere refers to the universal offering of salvation to all men).

God's response to Paul's request is unknown to us, yet his dependence upon *prayer* as a means of accomplishing it is remarkable. Thus, we are not only to ask, seek, and knock (in prayer) for ourselves, but also for others who fulfill the cause of Christ (Mat. 7:7–8). "[T]hat I may make it clear in the way I ought to speak" (4:4)—i.e., instead of relying on his own talents or personal knowledge, Paul asks for divine help through the petitions of fellow believers (cf. 1 Cor. 2:1–5). The words "make it clear" indicates a twofold request: first, that Paul would be clear in his communication of the message; second, that the message would be clearly understood by those who received it.

Expected Christian Conduct and Speech (4:5–6): "Conduct yourselves with wisdom [or, Walk with wisdom—KJV]" (4:5)—this general instruction is covered in Eph. 5:15–17, yet here it has a more specific purpose: "toward outsiders." These "outsiders" are undoubtedly those outside of the body of Christ—those not yet redeemed by the blood of Christ (recall 1:13–14). The believer is to exercise wisdom, discretion, and maturity in how he behaves in the company of unbelievers, and especially when he shares the gospel with them. He is to speak the truth, to be sure, but he is to do so "in love" (Eph. 4:15). The Christian's objective is not only to survive this life with his faith intact, but also to *live* his faith as a godly influence to others (Mat. 5:16) and to *share* his faith in hopes that others might hear and repent (see 2 Tim. 2:24–26). Hendriksen has something worthwhile to say on this:

> In the days of the early church believers were often slandered by these outsiders. For example, they were called *atheists* because they served no visible gods, *unpatriotic* because they did not burn incense before the image of the emperor, and *immoral* because, of necessity, they would often meet behind locked doors. The apostle knew that the best way to defeat this

> slander was for Christians daily to conduct themselves not only *virtuously* instead of *wickedly* but also *wisely* instead of *foolishly*. … It was then as it is now: in the long run the reputation of the gospel depends on the conduct of its devotees.[190]

"[M]aking the most of the opportunity" means taking advantage of the moment and realizing the importance of the message that needs to be communicated. Such "opportunity" may not always be comfortable or convenient, but one must seize it when it arises—and in many cases, we must vigilantly *seek* opportunity rather than waiting for it to present itself obviously to us. The Greek text is translated as "redeeming the time," which (consistent with the act of redemption) involves buying back a "time" that could have been lost or used for some lesser purpose (as in Eph. 5:16). (It also implies being productive *with* our time, but the "redemption" idea is often lost on us.)

In conjunction with our proper conduct before outsiders, we must watch what we say—and how we say it (4:6). A person's words reflect what is in his heart or indicate what drives his thinking (Mat. 15:17–20, 1 Peter 4:11). A Christian's words ought to reflect the influence and guidance of the Holy Spirit, to be full of grace. "Grace" here cannot mean *saving* grace (since only God can impart this to anyone) but that which is kind, beneficial, and generous (as is God's benevolence toward wicked men). "Salt" is a flavoring agent as well as a preservative. In the Levitical sacrifices, the "covenant of salt" symbolized the preservation of one's relationship with God (Lev. 2:13, Num. 18:19). Likewise, our words are to be a source of inspiration (or flavor) as well as timeless quality (or preservation), especially to "outsiders" who are seeking the truth. Our response to each person should be already prepared in our heart and conditioned by our desire for the salvation of all men (1 Peter 3:15, 1 Tim. 2:3–4).

---

190 Hendriksen, *NTC*, 182; all emphases are his.

Paul's Personal Circumstances and Salutations (Col. 4:7–18)

Not everything Paul wants to say—in the way of instruction or as to his personal circumstances—is in this epistle. His loyal assistants, Tychicus and Onesimus, will bring the rest of this information to the Colossians personally (4:7–9). It is believed that Tychicus was the actual bearer of this epistle to Colossae, just as he was the bearer of the epistle to Ephesus (Eph. 6:21–22). He is mentioned several other times in the NT, always in a positive light (Acts 20:4, 2 Tim. 4:12, and Titus 3:12); even here, he is highly praised as a "faithful and beloved brother." In Acts 20:4, Tychicus (and Trophimus) are identified as being "from [the province of] Asia," making Tychicus a native of the general region to which Colossae and Ephesus belong.

Likewise, Onesimus is a native of Colossae, and would be well familiar with the area. Both men would bring further details of Paul's imprisonment, as well as the progress of his legal affairs, which would be of great interest to the Colossians. In the next verses, six other men are mentioned, some with whom we are familiar elsewhere and others about whom we know nothing else than these brief words (4:10–15).

- **Aristarchus:** A Macedonian from Thessalonica (Acts 20:4), this man has had a colorful history with Paul so far. He is Paul's fellow worker (Phile. 1:24) as well as his fellow prisoner. He was arrested along with Gaius in Ephesus (Acts 19:23ff); he was with Paul on his ill-fated voyage to Rome (Acts 27:2); and it appears he is literally imprisoned at the same time as Paul. (Some commentators suggest that some of Paul's friends voluntarily shared imprisonment with him, and that this explains the reference made in 4:10.)
- **Mark:** This is John Mark, Barnabas' cousin, the author of the gospel called by his name. Early in Paul's missionary endeavors, Mark had abandoned him, leaving a sour taste in Paul's mouth regarding his reliability (compare Acts 13:13 and 15:36–40). Later, however, it seems Mark has matured in his faith and thus has become very useful to Paul (2 Tim. 4:11, Phile. 1:24).

- ❏ **"Jesus, who is called Justus"**: Nothing else is known of this man, save that he is willing to minister to the Gentiles. "Jesus" is his Hebrew name; "Justus" is his Latinized (Roman) name. Aristarchus, Mark, and Justus are "from the circumcision" (i.e., are pure-blooded Jews who have become Christians), and have served as a source of encouragement for Paul. Many other Jews have abandoned Paul. "The Greek [text] indicates comfort in the dangers of discussion or debate; a different word is used to mean comfort with respect to internal problems."[191] The fact that these first three men are identified as "from the circumcision" indicates that the following three men are Gentiles.
- ❏ **Epaphras**: This man is considered the founder of the church in Colossae (recall 1:7); thus, he is "one of your number." At the time of writing, he is with Paul in Rome, and possibly serves as a fellow inmate with him at times (Phile. 1:23). Epaphras shows great concern for his home church and labors diligently on its behalf, wanting to see the Christians there come to maturity and completion (recall 1:28–29). Laodicea and Hierapolis are nearby sister cities to Colossae, and Epaphras may have also founded churches there. Laodicea was named after Laodike, queen of Antiochus II (261–246 BC), and is regarded as the "chiefest city" of Phrygia. It became especially famous (and wealthy) because of its production of fine black wool and for a healing powder (or salve) for the eyes (see Rev. 3:18). Hierapolis is six miles north of Laodicea and twelve miles from Colossae. According to tradition, Philip the evangelist first preached the gospel there, and was buried there along with two of his unmarried daughters. Once the seat of staunch paganism, it became instead a center of Christian worship for centuries. In AD 62, soon after the writing of this epistle, an earthquake destroyed all three cities. Laodicea, for its part, rebuilt itself with the wealth of its own citizens, spurning financial aid offered by Rome.[192]
- ❏ **"Luke, the beloved physician"**: A Gentile who became one of the greatest historians of the early church, Luke has provided an

---

191 JFB, *Commentary* (electronic), on 4:11; bracketed word is mine.
192 *Ibid.*, on 4:13; E. J. Banks, "Hierapolis" and "Laodicea," *ISBE* (electronic).

invaluable service to Paul's ministry. He is the author of the gospel account by his name, it being the result of great research and investigation on his part (Luke 1:1–4). Though not mentioned by name in *Acts*, he is nonetheless the author of that work as well as a participant in its narrative (in the infamous "we" sections—Acts 16:10, 20:6, 27:1, etc.). Luke is a gifted writer, well-educated, and a keen observer of details—and especially of historical details (see Luke 3:1–2, for example). He is also a dear and loyal friend of Paul's, having accompanied him on his voyage to Rome and his imprisonment there. He will also be with Paul in his final imprisonment (2 Tim. 4:11). There is credible evidence to believe that Luke and Titus are biological brothers.[193]

- **Demas:** Here (and in Phile. 1:24), Demas is identified as one of Paul's fellow workers. In 2 Tim. 4:10, however, we find that he will abandon Paul, "having loved this present world." We know nothing else about this man, and yet it appears that he finds greater gratification in "this present world" than he does in serving alongside one of the greatest men in Christ's church.

"[T]he brethren who are in Laodicea" and "the church that is in [Nympha's] house" (4:15) clearly refer to two groups. Likely, one is the main (or larger) congregation within the city; the other is a smaller group meeting in someone's home. The Greek wording in this sentence is irregular, giving rise to various interpretations, but the conclusion offered here seems to be the most natural and straightforward. It is impossible without any further information, however, to determine from the Greek whether "Nympha" is feminine or masculine. Thus, all we know about her (or him) and the church at her (or his) home is what Paul wrote here.

"The letter {that is coming} from Laodicea" (4:16) appears to be a circular letter (or general epistle) that is to be read in several churches, just as *Colossians* was to be read to more than just the Colossians themselves. It has been suggested that the Laodicean letter is what we call *Ephesians*, but there is no conclusive evidence for this. "Say

---

193 A. T. Robertson, "Luke the evangelist," *ISBE* (electronic).

to Archippus … " (4:17)—Paul singles this man out for special encouragement, like what we find in Phil. 4:2–3. He is mentioned in Phile. 1:2 only as a "fellow soldier"; otherwise, we know nothing else about him or his circumstances other than what is written here. It seems apparent, however, that Paul wants him to fulfill the ministry to which he once committed himself (cf. 2 Tim. 4:5).

"I, Paul, write … hand"—though Paul did not personally pen this entire letter, this signature closure indicates that he is nonetheless its author (4:18; see 1 Cor. 16:21, Gal. 6:11, and 2 Thess. 3:17). It was common for him to dictate his letters to an *amanuensis*, what we would call a scribe or secretary today. "Remember my imprisonment"—something that Christians ought to do for all fellow brothers or sisters imprisoned for their faith (Heb. 13:3). "This last reminder would again bring them to consider how he had struggled for them even while in chains and written an epistle to liberate them from erring theology and point them back to Christ as supreme."[194] "Grace be with you"—in essence, "May God continue to impart His grace to you, as those who are called by Him."

---

194 JFB, *Commentary* (electronic), on 4:18.

Sources Used for *Colossians*

Barnes, Albert. *Barnes' Notes*, vol. 12. Grand Rapids: Baker Book House, no date.

Boren, Henry C. *Roman Society*, 2nd ed. Lexington, MA: Heath and Co., 1992.

Bruce, F. F. "Commentary on the Epistle to the Colossians." *The New International Commentary on the New Testament: The Epistles to the Ephesians and Colossians*. Grand Rapids: Wm. B. Eerdmans Publishing Co., 1979.

Coffman, James Burton. *Commentary on Galatians, Ephesians, Philippians, Colossians*. Austin, TX: Firm Foundation, 1977.

Cogdill, Roy E. *The New Testament: Book by Book*. Marion, IN: Cogdill Foundation Publications, 1975.

Geisler, Norman L. *Christian Apologetics*. Grand Rapids: Baker Book House, 1976.

Hendriksen, William. *New Testament Commentary: Galatians, Ephesians, Philippians, Colossians and Philemon*. Grand Rapids: Baker Books, 1995.

International Standard Bible Encyclopedia, electronic edition. © 1979 by Wm. B. Eerdmans Publishing Co.; database © 2013 by WORDsearch Corp.

Jamieson, Robert, Andrew Fausset and David Brown. *Jamieson, Fausset, and Brown Commentary: Commentary Critical and Explanatory on the Whole Bible (1871)*, electronic edition. Database © 2012 by WORDsearch Corp.

Lenski, R. C. H. *Commentary on the New Testament, vol. 9: The Interpretation of St. Paul's Epistles to the Colossians, to the Thessalonians, to Timothy, to Titus, and to Philemon*. Peabody, MA: Hendrickson Publishers, 1998.

Lipscomb, David. *A Commentary on the New Testament Epistles, volume IV: Ephesians, Philippians and Colossians*. J. W. Shepherd, ed. Nashville: Gospel Advocate Co., 1976.

Robertson, Archibald T. *Word Pictures in the New Testament*, vol. 4. Grand Rapids: Baker Books, 1931.

Strong, James. *Strong's Talking Greek–Hebrew Dictionary*, electronic edition. Database © WORDsearch Corp.

Sychtysz, Chad. *The Holy Spirit of God: A Biblical Perspective.* Waynesville, OH: Spiritbuilding Publishers, 2010.

Thayer, Joseph. *Thayer's Greek–English Lexicon*, electronic edition. Database © 2014 by WORDsearch Corp.

Vincent, Marvin. *Word Studies*, electronic edition. Database © 2014 by WORDsearch Corp.

∽ **End of *Quick Study Commentary: Colossians*** ∽

www.ingramcontent.com/pod-product-compliance
Lightning Source LLC
Chambersburg PA
CBHW041925090426
42743CB00020B/3441